Contents

Acknowledgments   vii

Note on References   viii

Introduction   1

1. The Accidental Irishman (1667–1707)   3

2. The Prince of Journalists (1707–1714)   36

3. The Hibernian Patriot (1714–1725)   61

4. The World-Besotted Traveller (1725–1727)   87

5. A Poisoned Rat in a Hole (1727–1745)   112

Postscript   141

References   144

Select Bibliography   146

Index   150

For Dominic, Patrick and Damian

JONATHAN SWIFT

BERNARD TUCKER

GILL AND MACMILLAN

First published 1983 by
Gill and Macmillan Ltd
Goldenbridge
Dublin 8
with associated companies in
Auckland, Dallas, Delhi,
Hong Kong, Johannesburg, Lagos,
London, Manzini, Melbourne, Nairobi,
New York, Singapore, Tokyo, Washington

available in this series:
Michael Collins (Leon Ó Broin)
Seán O'Casey (Hugh Hunt)
C. S. Parnell (Paul Bew)
James Craig (Patrick Buckland)
James Joyce (Peter Costello)
Eamon de Valera (T. Ryle Dwyer)
Daniel O'Connell (Fergus O'Ferrall)
Theobald Wolfe Tone (Henry Boylan)
Edward Carson (A. T. Q. Stewart)
James Connolly (Ruth Dudley Edwards)
Arthur Griffith (Calton Younger)
Jonathan Swift (Bernard Tucker)
George Bernard Shaw (John O'Donovan)
Oscar Wilde (Richard Pine)
Seán Lemass (Brian Farrell)
W. B. Yeats (Augustine Martin)

Origination by Galaxy Reproductions Ltd, Dublin
Printed in Hong Kong

Acknowledgments

I have quoted fairly extensively from Swift's own work and especially from his letters, which tell us more about him than critics often can. However, anyone who writes about Swift is indebted to Irvin Ehrenpreis's scholarly two volumes of biography, which take Swift's life up to 1714. It would also be difficult to write about Swift without acknowledging the many challenging books on different aspects of his work, and these are listed in the bibliography. I am indebted to these writers for their illumination of Swift.

While preparing this book I was grateful to Patrick Reilly of Glasgow University for letting me see a draft of his book on Swift, which had not then been published. It seems to provide an exciting and fresh examination of Swift's work.

I would like to thank those who have helped me with the book, either directly or indirectly: Warren Chernaik, Janet Woolf and Linda Stubbs. Special thanks are due to James Sambrook, whose eagle eyes saved me considerable embarrassment. Above all, I am indebted to the four wise men, colleagues and friends, who acted as Swift's servants did for his work and, having read the draft of the book, made countless invaluable suggestions: Paul Gardner, Peter Barry, Brendan Jackson, and our *primus inter pares*, who retired before we wanted him to, Tom Buck.

NOTE ON REFERENCES

Quotations from the *Prose Writings of Jonathan Swift* are referenced in parentheses by volume number (I-XIV) followed by page number(s). Quotations from *The Correspondence of Jonathan Swift* are referenced in parentheses by volume number (i-v) followed by page number(s). Quotations from *The Poetry of Jonathan Swift* are referenced in parentheses by volume number (I-III) followed by page number(s). Quotations from *Journal to Stella* are referenced in parentheses by 'JS' followed by volume number (I-II) and page number(s). Quotations from *Books about Swift*, listed in the Bibliography, see pp. 146-49, are referenced by the same number, italicised, as introduces each one in the Bibliography, followed by page number(s), in parentheses. Thus the reference *(8*, 44) would show that the preceding quotation is from Louis A. Landa's *Swift and the Church of Ireland*.

Quotations from sources other than these are detailed in the reference notes, p. 144-5, each one of which can be traced back to a corresponding superscript number in the relevant chapter of text.

Introduction

'Will the real Jonathan Swift please stand up?' is the despairing question which haunts anyone writing about this most complex and paradoxical figure. He lived in an age of disguises and hardly ever wrote as 'Jonathan Swift'. Despite a lifetime of writing and preaching, he usually succeeded in concealing his real self. We can search his work and still be no wiser about him. Nor can we be any more sure about Lemuel Gulliver, Isaac Bickerstaff, M.B. Drapier, Simon Wagstaff, or any of the other personalities Swift assumed. Just when we feel we have him cornered he escapes.

We will never understand why a man who wrote so straightforwardly (his letters as well as his prose and poetry are models of clarity) should have taken so much pleasure in riddles and disguises. It has been suggested that he feared rejection and so retained the escape-hatch of pseudonym and anonymity through which he could take refuge from dismissive criticism.

It is not easy to do justice to his personality in a small book, nor can one hope to throw any new light on the many puzzles about the events of his life. Critics have explored his satire, and his major prose works have received considerable attention. His vast correspondence would repay further study, although even here one senses a self-dramatisation as he seems so often to tailor his mood to the recipient of the letter; his poetry is now seen to be worth serious

discussion. Aspects of his personality have been
[2] thoroughly examined and some have tried to
penetrate the mysteries of his relationships with
Stella and Vanessa.

With some writers we can follow their lives and see
how their ideas and philosophies developed: but
Swift defies this approach. His ideas were formed
early in his life and, in some cases, inherited from
those who went before him; he hardly changed them
throughout his life. His later Irish writings are an
extension of what he wrote early in the century, the
objects of his satire in *Gulliver's Travels* are those of
all his work in poetry and prose, the techniques he
used early on are still present in his last writing; his
poetry shows none of the development we see in
Pope, for example, working from early *Pastorals* to
later *Dunciad*. However, the major concerns of all his
work are not really with the trivia of the passing
political scene, with church politics nor even with
Ireland's struggle against English oppression. He was
concerned to go to the root of all these problems and
to make men look at those timeless things which he
felt were the causes: man's pride and self-deception,
the prevalence of hypocrisy and injustice, the activities
of fools and knaves. These are still with us today.

1
The Accidental Irishman

Jonathan Swift was born in Dublin on 30 November 1667 in Hoey's Court near St Werburgh's Street in what was then one of the best neighbourhoods of Dublin and also the area where leading lawyers lived. Dublin was a prosperous city between 30,000 and 40,000 people, second only in size to London in the British Isles and considered one of the first half dozen cities in Western Europe. His parents were English, although his mother had probably been born in Ireland where her parents emigrated in 1634. She married Jonathan Swift the elder in 1664, after he had crossed to Ireland with his three brothers at the time of the Restoration of Charles II. He had a post in the King's Inns in Dublin and so, like two of his brothers, had connections with the legal profession. The brothers were helped by influential patrons, since they were related to the Duke of Ormonde through his wife, and they were also helped by Sir John Temple, Master of the Rolls, the father of Sir William Temple, who later became the patron of the younger Jonathan Swift. In addition to useful patrons, Swift's parents had literary connections, for his uncle Thomas had married the daughter of Sir William Davenant the poet and Swift was himself second cousin once removed to John Dryden, the most important literary figure of the later seventeenth century.

Although he claimed that his relations were 'of all mortals what I most despise and hate' (v, 137-8),

Swift made much of his relationship to Dryden. In
[4] addition he benefited from the circumstances of his
birth into an Anglo-Irish family which took economic
advantage of the peace in Ireland following the
upheaval of the Commonwealth period. He was not
unlike Yeats in his devotion to selected ancestors, in
his case the Reverend Thomas Swift, Vicar of
Goodrich and Rector of Bridstow in Herefordshire.
This royalist grandfather had suffered considerably
from the Puritans under Cromwell, having been, in
Swift's words, 'persecuted and plundered two and
fifty times by the barbarity of Cromwell's hellish
crew' (v, 150). He had been ejected from two parishes
in 1646, imprisoned for a time in Raglan Castle and
suffered the theft of property. Swift himself inherited
the political and religious alignments of his father and
his grandfather, which were, not surprisingly, high
church Anglican and anti-Whig and he maintained
these throughout his life in one form or other.

Jonathan Swift the elder died in March or April
1667, seven or eight months before his son's birth,
leaving his widow dependent on the generosity of her
brothers-in-law. It is not surprising that Swift later had
considerable reservations about marriage, as one sees
from his comments on that of his own parents:

> This marriage was on both sides very indiscreet, for
> his wife brought her husband little or no fortune,
> and his death happening so suddenly before he
> could make a sufficient establishment for his family:
> and his son (not then born) has often been heard
> to say that he felt the consequences of that marriage
> not only through the whole course of his education,
> but during the greatest part of his life (v, 192).

He was thus left with his mother, and it is here that
the many mysteries surrounding his life begin. He
always referred to her as a woman of great virtue

and usually made a point of visiting her at Leicester when he was *en route* between London and Ireland. [5] But there is the mystery of his being 'kidnapped' by his nurse, who took him to her native Cumberland and kept him there for three years. He wrote of the incident when he was an old man and conveniently vague about events in his early days and there are inconsistencies in his story. The events certainly underpinned his ambivalent attitude to his Irish identity, since he wrote that 'I happened indeed by a perfect accident to be born here [i.e. in Ireland]' (iv, 229), and complained of 'my banishment in this miserable country' (iv, 126).

The nurse certainly looked after her young charge and taught him to read. At the age of six he was sent to the excellent grammar school in Kilkenny, which had been founded by the influential Ormonde family. Mrs Swift moved to Leicester with her daughter Jane, who married a tradesman in 1699, beneath Swift's expectations and in spite of his opposition, and he probably only saw his mother once more up to the time he left university. Although he grew up with very little maternal contact and no contact at all with a father, none of his early biographers thought it necessary to comment on this aspect of his upbringing and one can only conclude that it was not uncommon at the time.

Kilkenny was the finest school of its kind in Ireland and much patronised by the 'Old English' gentry of the Pale (that area around Dublin so long inhabited by English settlers). Among its former pupils were Peter Lombard, the historian and Catholic Archbishop of Armagh, and Luke Wadding, the Franciscan scholar and exiled Irish Catholic patriot. Here Swift was given the traditional grounding in Greek, Latin, religion, public speaking and writing. It was probably here that he first learnt to play with words and to indulge in the

linguistic puzzles which lasted throughout his life. He
[6] spent eight years in Kilkenny School, living in an
entirely masculine society, and then in 1682 at the
age of fourteen proceeded to another masculine
institution, Trinity College of the University of Dublin.

Trinity College was also under the patronage of the
Dukes of Ormonde and its chief role at the time was
to provide clergy for the Church of Ireland. Here Swift
came under the influence of his tutor and subsequently
lifelong friend, the slightly older St George Ashe. Ashe
was a mathematician and experimental philosopher,
who was extremely active in the Dublin Philosophical
Society, and it is quite likely that Swift's portrayal of
the Academicians in Book Three of *Gulliver's Travels*
had its origins in his friend's researches. At Trinity
College, where most of the instruction was by lectures
in Latin, Swift followed the normal course of studies.
The content of the B.A. course was chiefly Latin,
Greek and Hebrew and the traditional Aristotelian
philosophy. In addition, students took part in disput-
ations couched in the form of syllogisms, a method
designed to demonstrate their understanding of
material. The curriculum, and particularly the syllog-
istic exercises, had a pronounced bearing on Swift's
subsequent writing, since the syllogism, correctly (or
sometimes incorrectly) applied, can be used to
humorous effect. He performed tolerably well at
university in Latin and Greek, but his early biographers
tell us that he had little time for Logic and Metaphysics, took note of Mathematics and Natural
Philosophy only to ridicule them and was really
interested only in History and Poetry. He had little
time for the Provost of Trinity, Narcissus Marsh, and
wrote of him in the ironic style he made his particular
forte: '[he] has the reputation of most profound and
universal learning; this is the general opinion, neither
can it be easily disproved. An old rusty iron chest in a

banker's shop, strongly locked and wonderfully heavy, is full of gold; this is the general opinion, neither can [7] it be disproved, provided the key be lost' (V, 211). Swift was granted his B.A. degree early in 1686, graduating 'by special grace'. This method of graduating was not uncommon at the time, but it does suggest that he was lucky to gain the degree at all, not because of academic weakness, but because of infringements of College rules. After graduating he stayed on for a further three years of study.

His behaviour as an undergraduate was not distinguished. He had a bad record for fines imposed for absences from chapel and classes and in March 1687 he was admonished for 'neglect of duties and frequenting of the town'. Later, he and others were found guilty of starting tumults in the College and insulting the Junior Dean, as a result of which he was ordered together with another student to beg the Junior Dean's pardon publicly on bended knees.

At this time Dublin, like England, was in a state of turmoil as the last months of James II's reign gave way to his abdication and the arrival of William III. Swift wrote in 1689, 'The troubles then breaking out, he went to his mother, who lived in Leicester, and after continuing there some months, he was received by Sir William Temple, whose father had been a great friend to the family, and who was now retired to his house called Moor Park in Surrey' (V, 193). Temple had passed a distinguished life as a diplomat, writer, traveller, man of taste and connoisseur. He was famous above all as the proponent of a Protestant alliance against France. He was also a friend of William III, who came down to visit him at Moor Park. Swift became his secretary, writing, reading aloud and keeping accounts. In addition, for the next twenty years or so he transcribed, edited and saw through the press virtually all Temple's literary works.

With two long breaks he lived for a decade in Temple's
[8] household and came to see him not only as a patron
but virtually as a father. In addition, it was at Moor
Park that he met the child of eight, Esther Johnson,
whom he nicknamed 'Stella' and who became his
closest companion until her death in 1728. He also
contracted the illness which remained with him for
the rest of his life: Ménière's disease, that disturbance
of the inner ear, which causes vertigo and deafness.
The aetiology of this illness was not ascertained until
1861, so Swift, not surprisingly, did not understand
that the various symptoms were all due to the same
cause and he traced his giddiness to an over-indulgence
in apples and his deafness to a cold: 'I got my
giddiness by eating a hundred golden pippins at a
time at Richmond . . . having made a fine seat about
twenty miles farther in Surrey, where I used to read
and sleep, there I got my deafness' (iii, 232). His
physicians suggested that the climate might also have
contributed to the disease, so after Temple had written
a letter of recommendation to Sir Robert Southwell,
who was going to Ireland with the King, Swift returned
there, probably stopping off at Leicester to visit his
mother. However, the Irish climate did not improve
his health, so at Temple's invitation he returned to
England about August 1691, staying with his mother
until the autumn. In 1692 he went to Oxford, was
incorporated at Hart Hall and with his cousin Thomas
was admitted to the M.A. degree in July.

At this time he started to write poetry, but it was
the rather solemn poetry of his half-a-dozen early
odes, which he wrote between 1690 and 1693, poems
of considerable length, dedicated to particular people
or written on specific occasions. Although there are
some indications of later poetic development in these
poems, he abandoned the ode and started writing
verse again only in 1698, after which he was usually

dismissive of his poetry: 'I have been only a man of rhymes, and that upon trifles, never having written [9] serious couplets in my life' (iv, 52), he wrote later. Quite often his poetry seemed to be almost deliberately *anti*-poetic as he made fun of the established practices of his contemporaries.

He spent the next two and a half years at Moor Park. In November 1692 he wrote to his Uncle William, 'I am not to take orders till the King gives me a prebendary; and Sir William Temple, though he promises me the certainty of it, yet is less forward than I could wish, because, I suppose, he believes I shall leave him and, upon some accounts, he thinks me a little necessary to him' (i, 12). Also in 1692 he had his first experience of courts when King William came down to ask Temple's advice about the Triennial Bill, as a result of which Temple sent Swift to the King with his views, which were ignored.

In May 1694 he decided to leave Moor Park, return to Ireland and take Holy Orders. Temple was not pleased as Swift reported: 'He was extremely angry I left him; and yet would not oblige himself any further than upon my good behaviour, nor would promise me any thing firmly at all, so that everybody judged I did best to leave him. I design to be ordained September next, and make what endeavours I can for something in the church' (i, 16). On his return to Ireland, finding that he needed a certificate of 'good life and behaviour' from Sir William, he wrote to Temple, who provided the required certificate and Swift was ordained priest by the Bishop of Kildare in Christ Church Cathedral Dublin in January 1695, obtaining the living of Kilroot near Belfast.

Swift spent the whole of his life in the Church of Ireland and all his efforts to achieve satisfactory advancement there were of no avail. The Church of Ireland was at this time in an enfeebled and ineffective state. Since so many of the population were Catholics [10] and many others, especially in the North, were Dissenters, there were consequently few worshippers in the Church of Ireland. The diocese of Ferns, for example, comprising virtually the whole county of Wexford, containing 131 parishes served by only thirteen priests and nine curates; neither bishop, dean nor archdeacon was resident in the diocese. The Church of Ireland survived only because it was supported by the English and Anglo-Irish landlords and other members of the Ascendancy, who used it as a means of retaining political power over Catholics and native Irish. Yet these landlords resented the payment of tithes to the Church and avoided paying them in every possible way.

Swift arrived in Kilroot in the declining days of the Primacy of Archbishop Michael Boyle, whom Ehrenpreis describes as 'a decayed octogenarian, senilely absent-minded, very hard of hearing, and nearly blind – an appropriate emblem of the Anglican establishment in Ireland' (1, 156). The parish of Kilroot comprised the union of the vicarages of Kilroot and Templecorran and the rectory of Balynure. The post carried with it the prebend of Kilroot in the cathedral of the diocese of Connor, which in 1662 had only seven churches in good repair out of sixty-seven. The county of Antrim, in which Kilroot lay, was reported in 1657 as having half its churches in ruins, a third with no resident clergy and its bishop, Thomas Hackett, was known as the Bishop of Hammersmith because of his prolonged residence in London. By the time Swift arrived, an ecclesiastical commission had investigated the diocese and had ordered 'suspensions, excommunications, and deprivations for such varied offences as drunkenness, fornication, adultery, neglect of cures, pluralism, diversion of funds, excessive procuration and visit-ation fees, non-residence, illegal use of the bishop's seal, and simony' (*8*, 13). There was no rectory attached to Swift's parishes and only a ruined church at Kilroot; his other churches were about eight miles apart and one of these was in poor repair. The parish contained many Scots planter Presbyterians and virtually no Catholics. However, Swift was lucky in having several well-connected people in the area. There was the Earl of Donegal in Carrickfergus, Richard Dobbs of Castle Dobbs, a former mayor of Carrickfergus and Henry Clements, like Dobbs, one of the churchwardens.

Swift became friendly with Jane Waring, who lived about thirty miles from Carrickfergus. He gave her the poetic nickname of 'Varina' and she became the first of the three fatherless young women with whom he was to form relationships. He eventually managed to extricate himself from a cautious friendship in which he had kept his options open and one can see why when one considers what he had written some four years earlier: 'I confess I have known one or two men of sense enough, who, inclined to frolics, have married and ruined themselves out of a maggot [that is, an infatuation]; but a thousand household thoughts, which always drive matrimony out of my mind whenever it chances to come there, will, I am sure, fright me from that' (i, 5).

He soon grew weary of Kilroot and in the spring of 1696 when Temple asked him to return to Moor Park he quickly agreed. While he had been absent his cousin Thomas had taken over his role, but had subsequently obtained a parish near Guildford. In addition, Lady Temple had died. Swift travelled from Kilroot via Belfast, Dublin and Holyhead, staying with his mother at Leicester and then moved on to Moor Park. He did not resign Kilroot for another eighteen months, being granted a licence of absence from his parishes,

extendible on request. Temple is reputed to have per-
[12] suaded him to give up Kilroot with the promise of an
English parish. Swift was now more confident in his
relationship with him and acted far more as literary
assistant, with the result that at this time his style
owes much to Temple since he transcribed and edited
hundreds of pages of his patron's writings.

On his return to Moor Park Swift found that the
child Esther Johnson was now a lively and intelligent
girl of fifteen. She was the daughter of Temple's
steward, who was now dead (although some have
asserted that she was actually Temple's illegitimate
daughter or even that Swift was her uncle) (3, 59).
Her companion was Rebecca Dingley, an unmarried
cousin of Temple's, who came of a good but impoverished family. She was known as 'Mrs' Dingley and
Swift usually wrote his letters to both women
together, never allowing himself to be alone with
Stella. Years later he summed up the Stella he met
at Moor Park:

> [he] had some share in her education, by directing
> what books she should read, and perpetually
> instructing her in the principles of honour and
> virtue; from which she never swerved in any one
> action or moment of her life. She was sickly from
> her childhood until about the age of fifteen; but
> then grew into perfect health, and was looked
> upon as one of the most beautiful, graceful and
> agreeable young women in London, only a little
> too fat. Her hair was blacker than a raven, and
> every feature of her face in perfection (V, 227).

This abstract is from Swift's *On the Death of Mrs
Johnson*, written soon after her death in 1728; so
the third person narration perhaps acts as an objective
mask for Swift to shelter behind. As he was almost
twice her age he could play the role of tutor, which

became his stock-in-trade in relationships with women. Although he continued to exchange letters with Varina he was now far more involved with Stella.

2

He had written no poetry at Moor Park following the lack of success of the early odes, dismissed by Dryden in the now immortal words', 'Cousin Swift you will never make a poet.' He did, however, write three prose works, *The Battle of the Books, The Mechanical Operation of the Spirit* and *A Tale of a Tub*, which, although closely related, are best discussed individually.

A Full and True Account of the Battle fought last Friday between the Ancient and the Modern books in Saint James's Library was written in 1697—8 and was prompted by an essay of Temple's in 1692 on ancient and modern learning, to which William Wotton had replied in favour of the moderns, so that the controversy spread, the Hon Charles Boyle for, and the critic Richard Bentley against the ancient writers. Swift pretended that the quarrel had spread to the books in Saint James's Library, of which Bentley was Curator. In true Swiftian style the result of the pitched battle was not known, since the 'Advertisement' tells us that 'the manuscript . . . by the injury of fortune, or weather, being in several places imperfect, we cannot learn to which side the victory fell' (I, 139).

Using Aesop's *Fables* and Phalaris's *Epistles* as evidence, Swift sets out to show the superiority of the ancients in prose. Authors are ranged humorously against each other: for the ancients 'Homer led the horse . . . Pluto and Aristotle commanded the bowmen' (I, 152), while Milton, Dryden, Tasso, Descartes and Hobbes were among the moderns. The medieval philosophers Scotus, Aquinas and Bellarmine [14] led 'a confused multitude . . . of mighty bulk and stature, but without either arms, courage, or discipline' (I, 152). Swift's 'cousin' Dryden makes a ludicrous appearance in combat with Virgil (whom he had translated), appearing in a helmet 'nine times too large for the head' (I, 157). The book also contains the famous fable of the Spider and the Bee. The spider with his love of dirt and self-sufficiency is the perfect modern, whereas the bee lives with the ancients, bringing home honey and wax, which produce sweetness and light.

The Battle of the Books is largely a personal satire against the critics Wotton and Bentley, but Swift also attacks the pedantry, clumsiness and distorted vision of modern writing in general. He delayed publishing it until 1704 and the reader is bound to ask why he went through with its publication. However, the essay is part of his general attack on moderns and he carried the attack more convincingly in the 'Satire on Learning' in *A Tale of a Tub*.

A Discourse concerning the Mechanical Operation of the Spirit is really a part of *A Tale of a Tub* which has been left standing on its own. It is a further examination of zeal or 'enthusiasm', which was under attack at the time since it was the mark of the Dissenters. The voice used for this work is that of the *virtuoso*, a scholar of the kind to be found in the Royal Society, always searching for new knowledge and discoveries and hence, to Swift's sceptical mind, always suspect. The use of a *virtuoso*, self-important and with limited vision, allows him ample scope for his views on contemporary philosophies and their followers.

'Good God! What a genius I had when I wrote that book,' said Swift years later about *A Tale of a Tub*, and this complicated, rambling cock-and-bull story is indeed one of his greatest achievements and a very necessary introduction to his work. He worked on the *Tale* for a decade and it made a great impact when published in the Spring of 1704, selling four editions in twelve months. In his 'Apology' of 1710 Swift gave an admirable summing up of the book when he wrote that the author of the tale 'thought the numerous and gross corruptions in religion and learning might furnish matters for a satire, that would be useful and diverting' (I, 1). The twofold theme of the book is a defence of the Church of England as the middle way between Catholicism and extreme Protestantism, and a satire on the corruption in learning brought about by the moderns. He is particularly hard on what he saw as the affectation and pedantry of seventeenth-century scholars, and many of his contemporaries; and even major philosophers such as Hobbes, are under fire in the book.

The tale itself is a fairly obvious allegory on the history of the Christian church. The father of triplets Peter (Catholicism), Martin (Anglicanism) and Jack (Calvinism) leaves each a coat in his will and strict instructions not to add nor subtract even a thread. The brothers find their unfashionable clothes are not acceptable to the world at large. Peter is the first to 'interpret' the will and justify addition to their coats of shoulder knots, satin, silk fringes and embroidery. The other two brothers quarrel with him when he hides the will and tries to dominate them before going mad. He throws them out of the house but they manage to take copies of the will, which they compare with the state of their own coats and realise how far they have strayed from the original. Martin removes as much as he can of the original material but is happy to leave additions if removing them would damage the basic coat itself. Jack is so anxious to restore the coat to its original state that he rips it; he becomes more concerned to remove any evidence of Peter's influence than to keep to the father's will. In the end [16] he goes mad and is obsessed with the wording of the will and its meaning.

Catholicism (Peter) is seen as having come too much to terms with the world, for it is now materially wealthy and has been corrupted by worldly standards. The Dissenting churches (Jack) have rejected the world in too extreme a fashion, insisted on too rigid a reading of the Bible and have accepted the doctrine of predestination so that there is no room for free will. Jack's stress on inspiration from the Holy Spirit led to the most celebrated part of the *Tale*, the description of the Aeolists, who 'maintain the original cause of all things to be wind, from which principle this whole universe was at first produced, and into which it must at last be resolved' (I, 95). Martin represents Anglicanism which has made a rational (perhaps Swift means 'sensible') compromise between Christianity and the material world. As Swift wrote of the *Tale* in the 'Apology', 'It celebrates the Church of England as the most perfect of all others in discipline and doctrine' (I, 2).

This rational Anglicanism was very much in the tradition of the seventeenth-century scholars whom Swift had read in his early days. They sought to integrate reason and revelation and make a rational basis for faith. However, there is considerable disagreement over Swift's position in this debate and it can be argued that he took up different positions depending on whether he was attacking Catholics or Dissenters. At the time that he was working on the *Tale* in the mid-1690s there was a serious revival of earlier schemes for Dissenters to join the Church of England, which he opposed, and in 1695 Locke's *The Reasonableness of Christianity* defined Christian revelation stripped of its mysteries and made it out to be entirely consistent with 'natural religion'. These developments are mirrored in the work. In addition to its defence of the Church of England, the *Tale* [17] ridicules confession, purgatory and transubstantiation at the Catholic extreme, and predestination, interminable prayers and opposition to vestments at the extreme of the Dissenters.

If the *Tale* consisted only of this religious allegory it might not have proved so difficult and confusing to readers over the years. However, interspersed with the allegory there are various digressions, five of which occur before the allegory begins; and a further, preliminary, digression came with the addition in 1710 of 'The Author's Apology' before the Dedication. The fable is interrupted by four digressions in which Swift parodies the bookseller's apparatus for padding useless pieces of writing to create a work of saleable size.

Another of the major complications of the *Tale* is the frequent difficulty posed by Swift's mouthpieces. The *Tale* has as many as five different spokesmen and behind these is Swift himself. The voice responsible for narrating most of the book is the 'Author', whom critics usually refer to as 'the Hack', a Grub Street hack, one of those literary drudges whom Swift and Pope pilloried so often. Panegyric was especially popular in poetry at the time and Swift had come to distrust it; this Hack prefers it to satire. Its exaggerated use of praise for a person or a set of ideas made panegyric especially suitable for parody and Swift enjoys mocking the Hack's enthusiastic praise with ironic results. In addition, the Hack shows himself to be a fraud, who is prepared to write for any cause so long as he is paid.

It is generally agreed that the 'Author's Apology' is written in Swift's own voice. This 'Author' reflects on the circumstances which caused him to write the book some thirteen years previously, when he was 'then young, his invention at the height, and his reading fresh in his head' (I, 1). He is anxious to [18] assure the reader that 'he had endeavoured to strip himself of as many real prejudices as he could' (I, 1). He goes on to make the kind of apology so frequently found in Swift's work: 'Some of those passages in this discourse which appear most liable to objection, are what they call parodies, where the author personates the style and manner of other writers whom he has a mind to expose' (I, 3). He is also at pains to stress that 'there generally runs an irony through the thread of the whole book, which the man of taste will observe and distinguish; and which will render some objections that have been made very weak and insignificant' (I, 4). Swift was always anxious to ensure that his point was not missed by the reader. If this apology really *is* unironical it does not finish on such a note because at the end of it we read a list of 'Treatises written by the same author, most of them mentioned in the following discourse, which will be speedily published'. This is followed by a list of eleven titles such as 'A general history of ears', 'A panegyrical essay upon the number three' and 'A modest defence of the proceedings of the rabble in all ages'.

The 'Bookseller's dedication' to Lord Somers is one of the finest examples of raillery that Swift ever wrote. 'Raillery' was much in fashion at the time and Swift used it to great effect in his letters and poems. He later defined it as 'to say something that at first appeared a reproach, or reflection; but, by some turn of wit unexpected and surprising, ended always in a compliment, and to the advantage of the person it was addressed to' (IV, 91). Despite Swift's attempts to spell things out, the greatest irony of the book is that so many people missed the point. *A Tale of a Tub* sets out many of the issues with which Swift was concerned throughout his life. It is about that conflict between illusion and reality which lends itself so readily to treatment through irony and which lay [19] behind all his work. Like *Gulliver's Travels* later and so many of his poems, the *Tale* is about that kind of pride 'when a man's fancy gets astride his reason, when imagination is at cuffs with the senses, and common understanding, as well as common sense, is kicked out of doors' (I, 108). Eighteenth-century denunciations of pride were often expressions of a certain disillusionment with mankind itself and pride was seen as a piece of excess human luggage to be dumped as quickly as possible. The ultimate denunciation of pride came in Swift's portrayal of the Gulliver. His whole life was devoted to preventing man getting above himself:

> Pray what is man, but a topsy turvy creature? His animal faculties perpetually mounted on his rational, his head where his heels should be, grovelling on the earth. And yet with all his faults he sets up to be a universal reformer and corrector of abuses, a remover of grievances, rakes into every slut's corner of nature, bringing hidden corruptions to the light, and raiseth a mighty dust where there was none before; sharing deeply all the while in the very same pollutions he pretends to sweep away (I, 240).

This is a clear forecast of the deeply pessimistic preoccupations often attributed to *Gulliver's Travels* and of his whole life: 'Life is a tragedy, wherein we sit as spectators awhile and then act out our part in it' (iii, 254). A further link with the *Travels* is the fact that worship of clothes in the religious allegory in *A Tale of a Tub* is an example of the worship of the *outside* of things. In the *Travels* Swift shocked many readers by forcing them to look beyond the surface to what lay underneath. This is also a concern

of many of his so-called 'scatological' poems. In *A*
[20] *Tale of a Tub* Swift writes with supreme irony, 'Last
week I saw a woman flayed, and you will hardly
believe how much is altered her person for the worse'
(I, 109).

In Section XI of *A Table of a Tub* his concern is
with madness, although the underlying preoccupation
is the *delusion* of happiness, which is described as
'a perpetual possession of being well deceived'.
Madness is a state in which we are subject to delusion
from inside and outside of ourselves. Our senses are
beset by a muddle of secondary qualities and phan-
toms ('the superficies of things'). Human happiness
depends on our self-deception; happiness is 'the serene
peaceful state of being a fool among knaves' (I, 110).
It is not only the madmen in Bedlam, but all of us
who are deceived. In devious fashion the Hack
advocates that the House of Commons should send
commissioners to Bedlam to inspect lunatics with a
view to giving them posts in the church and state
suited to their talents.

A great deal has been written about *A Tale of a
Tub* and few would claim to have grasped for long
the very complex and shifting nature of this unique
work.

3.

At this time Swift's contemporaries were flourishing.
The poet Matthew Prior was involved in international
diplomacy, while Swift's school- and college-mate
William Congreve had begun to establish himself as a
playwright. Addison had already achieved the foundation of his literary fame and his friend, the Irishman
Steele, was advancing his career. All these had the luck
or good sense to attach themselves to up-and-coming
patrons, whereas Swift had remained loyal to a man

who was becoming something of a figure from the past. In addition, he had made some errors of political judgment in approaching potential patrons. He had, for example, hopes of the Earl of Sunderland, the Lord Chamberlain, but Sunderland fell from office and Swift's hopes with him.

In January 1699 Temple died and Swift paid tribute to his many qualities. He also took the opportunity to set out his thoughts in 'When I come to be old 1699':

Not to marry a young woman. Not to keep young company unless they really desire it. Not to be peevish or morose or suspicious . . . Not to be fond of children (or let them come near me hardly). Not to tell the same story over and over again to the same people . . . Not to neglect decency or cleanliness, for fear of falling into nastiness. Not to be over severe with young people, but give allowance for their youthful follies and weaknesses. Not to be influenced by, or give ear to knavish tattling servants or others. Not to be too free of advice nor trouble any but those that desire it . . . Not to set up for observing all these rules, for fear I should observe none (I, xxxvii).

Temple, however, failed to provide for Swift, who immediately went up to London to promote his claims to the King for a prebend at Canterbury or Westminster, as Temple had promised; but he was unsuccessful. Temple left Swift £100 together with the task of publishing his literary remains. He now decided that his future lay in Ireland and he took the modest post of private chaplain to the new Lord Justice of Ireland, the Earl of Berkeley, sailing with him from Bristol to Dublin in August 1699.

Swift greatly enjoyed his life with the Berkeley family and his tasks as chaplain were not very taxing. He had a good deal of time to indulge in his enjoy-

ment of social conversation, reading, writing essays
and some light verse. He lived with the family in Dublin Castle and no doubt hoped that some kind of church promotion would shortly come his way. While with them he wrote an amazing poetic *tour de force* in the guise of one of Lady Betty Berkeley's gentlewomen, 'To their Excellencies the Lord Justice of Ireland the Humble Petition of Frances Harris, who must Starve, and Die a Maid if it miscarries'. He sustains the voice of this garrulous lady for seventy-five lines and shows in what at first seems mere doggerel his verbal dexterity and his excellent ear for the nuances of everyday speech:

> And, God knows, I thought my money was as safe
> as my maidenhead.
> So when I came up again, I found my pocket feel
> very light,
> But when I searched and missed my purse, Lord!
> I thought I should have sunk outright:
> Lord! Madam, says Mary, how d'ye do? Indeed,
> said I, never worse;
> But pray, Mary, can you tell what I have done
> with my purse!
> Lord help me, said Mary, I never stirred out of this
> place!
> Nay, said I, I had it in Lady Betty's chamber, that's
> a plain case (I, 69-70).

In January 1700 the Dean of Derry died and Swift felt sure that he would be given this wealthy deanery. Unfortunately for him, two of the most important figures in the decision were Narcissus Marsh, the former Provost of Trinity College (who had insisted on Swift providing the certificate of respectability before ordination) and the Bishop of Derry, William King, a former opponent of James II and a future Archbishop of Dublin. Not surprisingly, neither of these appears to have considered Swift, who later looked back in anger at the event:

In some months the deanery of Derry fell vacant and it was the Earl of Berkeley's turn to dispose of it. Yet things were so ordered that the secretary having received a bribe the deanery was disposed of to another and Mr Swift was put off with some other church-livings not worth above a third part of that rich deanery, and at this present time not worth a sixth. The excuse pretended was his being too young, although he were then thirty years old (V, 195).

However, he did manage to gain some pickings indirectly from the lost deanery. He received part of the former post of the new Dean of Derry, William Bolton, and became Vicar of Laracor and Rathbeggar and Rector of Agher, collectively known as Laracor. He also received Bolton's prebendary stall in St Patrick's Cathedral, thus marking the beginning of a connection with the Cathedral which continued until his death. The parishes covered ten square miles in Meath, some fifteen miles north-west of Dublin, that is, less than a half day's travel. There were no worshippers in Rathbeggar and few or none in Agher, but sixteen families, some of them very rich, lived in Laracor. The attendance at church was so low that on some occasions Swift preached to a congregation consisting only of his churchwarden, beginning his sermons 'Dearly beloved Roger'. His income was £230 a year, out of which he had to pay for curates to take his place during his frequent absences. This income was quite considerable when compared with that of other clergy, since only half a dozen rural clergy in the Dublin diocese had incomes over £100 per annum. He was presented to Laracor in February 1700 but put off until June his formal introduction to the living. He did not take an active part in diocesan [24] affairs and only attended cathedral chapter meetings thirteen times between 1702 and 1712. He was now, however, in a position to tap the upper levels of political influence, since he was in regular contact with the hierarchy of the Church of Ireland.

In 1700 Varina attempted to re-open their friendship and Swift replied in a cautious and almost devious way, protesting 'neither had I ever thoughts of being married to any other person but yourself' (i, 33), and he also presented a number of obstacles centred on her health and his income. He tried to let her down gently and sought to reassure her that what was happening was in some degree her fault: 'All I had in answer from you, was nothing but a great deal of arguing, and sometimes in a style so very imperious as I thought might have been spared, when I reflected how much you had been in the wrong' (i, 33). He concluded his letter (after saying he was too busy to visit the North) in a way which finally ended the relationship:

> I desire, therefore, you will let me know if your health be otherwise than it was when you told me the doctors advised you against marriage . . . Are you in a condition to manage domestic affairs, with an income of less (perhaps) than three hundred pounds a year? Have you such an inclination to my person and humour as to comply with my desires and way of living, and endeavour to make us both as happy as you can? Will you be ready to engage in those methods I shall direct for the improvement of your mind, so as to make us entertaining company for each other . . . Can you bend your love and esteem and indifference to others the same way as I do mine? (i, 35-6).

Varina remained unmarried and died many years before Swift.

He managed to visit England in 1701 and the following three years. In April 1701 he returned to England with Berkeley, who had been replaced by Lord Rochester, and paid his annual visit to his mother in Leicester. In London he was concerned with historical research, but interrupted this in order to produce an anonymous pamphlet, *A Discourse of the Contests and Dissensions between the Nobles and the Commons in Athens and Rome*, which was published in the Autumn of 1701. This was a defence of four leading Whig peers against the attack of the Tory majority in the Commons.

The *Discourse* is not ironic in tone and was published with the explicit intention of striking a blow for the Whig cause which he espoused at the time. In it he presented a review of constitutional history since the Conquest, following the general spirit of post-Revolution England. The theory then obtaining was that of contract: men gave up their liberties in order to enjoy peace and security in a disciplined state under a ruler whom they reserved the right to reject.

Although the pamphlet is of only limited interest to readers today it shows not only his attitude at the time, but his chief preoccupations, which changed little with his later move from Whig supporter to chief propagandist for the Tory Ministry. In particular, the *Discourse* shows his total commitment to the principles of the 'Glorious Revolution' of 1688 and to the way that he tended to analyse political activity in a pragmatic manner. It shows too, his attitude to party spirit, his ideal of liberty and his belief in the need to preserve personal freedom against all forms of despotic rule. Most notably, in this his earliest pamphlet, he displays his early aptitude for presenting propaganda through rhetorical devices.

[26]   At this time Swift was not a fanatical Whig, but he did accept the Revolution of 1688, which had replaced James II by William III, rightly, as he saw it, because James had broken his contract to rule justly. So he tended in politics to be a Whig, since the Whigs supported the theory that kings ruled by contract, whereas the Tories still clung somewhat precariously to the concept of Divine Right and some even remained sympathetic to the Stuart Pretender. In religion, however, he was a Tory churchman of the 1662 Act of Uniformity, since he saw the Tories as continuing and supporting the privileges of the Church of England. He retained these essential fundamental attitudes throughout his life. The Anglican monopoly of authorised worship had been broken by the Toleration Act of 1689, which allowed Protestant Dissenters who believed in the Trinity to worship in their own churches and chapels. A number of Dissenters were practising 'occasional conformity' and only attending Anglican worship on the minimum number of occasions specified by law and so they qualified for political office, thus destroying the Anglican monopoly of political power. Dissenters were therefore escaping the net of the two acts passed in Charles I's reign, the Corporation Act and the Test Act, which were supposed to keep them out of office. The Corporation Act required all members of borough corporations to receive communion in the Church of England at least once in the year before being appointed, which meant in effect an annual participation in the Church of England communion liturgy. The Test Act required those appointed to office under the Crown to receive communion within three months of being appointed. Occasional conformity was strongly opposed by the Tories, who tried to end the practice, while the Whigs,

sympathetic to the Dissenters, opposed any change. So Swift's opposition to any relaxation in the laws concerning conformity to the Church of England was not based so much on religious intolerance as on political expediency. As it turned out subsequently, events proved Swift wrong when the laws were relaxed.

Swift saw a good deal of Stella in the early summer of 1701 and tried to persuade her to move to Dublin to live near him. At this time he was thirty-four and she was twenty. Stella would, of course, rise in rank by moving to Dublin and, in addition, Temple had left her a lease of lands in Ireland worth £1,000 as well as other income. Mrs Dingley was prepared to accompany her to Ireland and so they arrived in Dublin in August. Swift was detained until September as he was returning with the new Lord Lieutenant, Rochester. Neither Stella nor Mrs Dingley left Ireland again except for one visit to England in 1708. The two ladies were introduced to Dublin society and always obtained lodgings near Swift whether he was at Laracor or in Dublin. He was anxious to avoid any hint of scandal and contrived, it is said, to meet Stella only in the presence of a third party (usually Mrs Dingley). With his habitual love of disguise he had already by 1701 grown into the habit of addressing Stella in letters as 'Ppt' (probably 'poppet'), Mrs Dingley as 'Dd' (probably 'Dear Dingley') and both together as 'Md' (probably 'My Dears'). He is 'Pdfr' ('poor dear foolish rogue') and all three friends are 'PMD'. But even these means could not prevent gossip, and his cousin Thomas asked six years later 'whether Jonathan be married or whether he has been able to resist the charms of both those gentlewomen that marched quite from Moor Park to Dublin (as they would have marched to the *north* or anywhere else) with full resolution to engage him?' (i, 56).

In February 1702 Swift took the degree of Doctor
of Divinity at Trinity College and kept himself busy editing more of Temple's manuscripts. But also in February King William III was thrown from his horse when it tripped on a molehill (the mole being the 'little gentleman in velvet' much toasted by exiled Jacobites) and he died on 8 March. The result of the death of the monarch, as Swift found later in 1714, was that all those in public positions had to look to their tenure. The Duke and Duchess of Marlborough were now closest to the new Queen Anne, whereas the Whigs led by Halifax and Somers were out of favour. Queen Anne was a staunch Anglican and took church appointments especially under her wing. Swift naturally hoped that his chances of ecclesiastical promotion would now increase and so he came to England in the second half of April, arriving in London from Leicester in May. He found that his *Contests and Dissensions* (published after he had left for Ireland) had been very well received and had run to two editions. During July he visited Moor Park and in August stayed with the Berkeleys in Gloucestershire, where he indulged in social life and wrote some amusing light verse. Throughout his life he wrote many light-hearted poems prompted by such occasions as visits to friends, slight disagreements and the peculiarities of people. An early, but not particularly outstanding example, is 'A Ballad on the Game of Traffick' of 1702. This card game, which needed a large number of players, took place at Berkeley Castle and the poem describes those taking part:

My Lady though she is no player
Some bungling partner takes,
And wedged in corner of a chair
Takes snuff, and holds the stakes . . .

"With these is Parson Swift,
"Not knowing how to spend his time,   [29]
"Does make a wretched shift,
"To deafen 'em with puns and rhyme." (I, 75)

Swift failed once again to obtain promotion and so, disappointed, he left the country in October 1702 and stayed in Ireland for twelve months.

5

In Ireland he busied himself at Laracor improving his small estate and repairing the church: 'My river walk is extremely pretty, and my canal in great beauty, and I see trout playing in it' (i, 373). There was little to occupy him at the ecclesiastical and political centres. In March 1703 William King became Archbishop of Dublin. He later became with Swift a leading Irish patriot in the affair of Wood's Half-pence, but everyone found him a difficult man to deal with. However, he was a fine example among his erring contemporaries and came to enjoy a relationship with Swift which was one of mutual respect between two strong characters. In November 1703 Swift returned to England along with other prominent people hurrying to London for the November meeting of Parliament.

In October 1703 the Dublin Parliament passed a number of ferocious acts against Catholics. Catholics could not lease land for more than thirty-one years; an estate might only descend to a man's sons by being equally divided between them, but if the eldest son declared himself a convert to the Church of Ireland he inherited the whole property. Then the Dublin Parliament followed the English example in passing the Test Act to Swift's approval and he published his first piece on Irish politics in defence of the Test, *A Letter from a Member of the House of Commons in*

Ireland to a Member of the House of Commons in
[30] *England concerning the Sacramental Test*, in
December 1708.

The Test Act became law in Ireland some months after Swift left, and he found the English Parliament obsessed with the same topic. He now made himself available to politicians in London and an invitation to join in the propaganda against the Occasional Conformity Bill resulted in his writing on the Whig side. He was to remain with the Whigs even while Robert Harley and Henry St John were gradually moving into position to form a Tory government.

About this time he set down his views on current politics, notably in *The Sentiments of a Church-of-England Man, with Respect to Religion and Government*, which was not published until 1711. The *Sentiments* is misleadingly titled since it contains Swift's views on constitutional matters as well as on church affairs. It is, in fact, the keystone of a number of pamphlets which he wrote on liberty in the opening decade of the century. Here he is particularly concerned with the relations between church and state. In addition to showing us his thinking at the time, the *Sentiments* looks forward to the views expressed in the *Drapier's Letters*, thus providing further evidence that his views on Ireland were the fruit of years of thinking and did not simply emerge after he had reluctantly settled there. His position on religion and government lay somewhere between the conservatism of the Tories and the radicalism of the Whigs. He was never a full supporter of those Tories who seemed to espouse the notion of the divine right of kings, and, as he had always accepted the concept of sovereignty as residing in the body of the people, he had never had any difficulty in accepting the succession to the throne which followed the Revolution of 1688 and the abdication of James II.

In the *Sentiments* Swift wanted to get his ideas straight. He felt conflicting loyalties between his support for the Whigs, which he felt was an inevitable consequence of his commitment to the principles of the Revolution, and his concern at their increasing hostility to the Church (as he saw their position). He presents himself, in an easy, almost conversational style, as a reasonable person, a moderate churchman, who wants to rise above party issues, who refuses to believe the popular parodies of party positions. As a result of being opposed to party factionalism and in favour of moderation, the Church of England Man indicates that the legislature is the all-powerful and important arm of government. The *Sentiments* concludes with the urging of a middle way: 'I should think that, in order to preserve the constitution entire in Church and State; whoever has a true value for both, would be sure to avoid the extremes of Whig for the sake of the former, and the extremes of Tory on account of the latter' (II, 225).

The *Sentiments* is made up of two parts, the first of which contains a non-partisan attitude towards religion and the second a similar treatment of government. In the first section Swift sums up the nature of the church and the place he felt it held in relation to the state. He deals with the place of dissent and shows that he was not (as many have felt) violently opposed to Dissenters but did feel unequivocally that they should not have positions of civil power; hence the necessity to maintain the Test Act. His position about Dissenters was always consistent. In his view, diversity of beliefs brought a practical danger to the ordered state and in addition, since men were normally disposed, he felt, substantially to agree, then marked differences of belief could only stem from irrational sources. There was never any extremism about his attitude to dissent.

In the second part of the essay he argues that one
[32] cannot lawfully resist the supreme magistrate under
any pretence whatsoever. He indicates that Hobbes was
mistaken and had confused the legislative power with
that of the executive: 'the administration cannot be
placed in too few hands, nor the legislature in too many'
(II, 18). He goes to considerable lengths to justify the
Revolution of 1688 and the succession of William of
Orange and sums up: 'the freedom of a nation consists
in an absolute unlimited legislative power, wherein the
whole body of the people are fairly represented, and
in an executive duly limited' (II, 23). This contains
the seed of his later concern with Ireland's freedom.

I have dealt at some length with the *Sentiments*
because it not only defines Swift's position in the
days when he was still a Whig, but also indicates
views which changed little over the years and became
the platform for his writings on Ireland.

As he waited for some improvement in his hopes
for promotion a new event occurred which gave him
a reason for remaining in London. In February 1704
Queen Anne finally agreed to give back to the Church
of England the fees traditionally paid to the Crown
by clergy and called 'First Fruits and Twentieth Parts'.
These fees would now be used to assist impoverished
livings in the Church of England. The convocation
of the Church of Ireland, anticipating this event
in its 1703—4 meetings (its first since 1666) sought
equal treatment from the Queen through the Bishop of
Cloyne. When the Bishop had to return to Ireland,
having received vaguely promising responses from the
Queen, Swift began to involve himself in the project. He
had quickly realised that such activity would enable him
to become well known to the important ministers of
state. However, it is important to state that he did not
see his role simply as a means of self-aggrandisement; he
genuinely believed that he could help his own church.

He could not afford to stay long in London and needed to be in Ireland if he were to keep open the chances of promotion in the church there, so calling on his mother *en route* he sailed for Ireland in May 1704. He now spent in Ireland three and a half not very productive years. During this time we can see the earliest written examples of his punning and playing with words, which he had begun while an undergraduate and which needed a highly receptive audience, which he discovered among his friends in Ireland. This punning and wordplay of Swift's has an obvious parallel in the writing of other, later Irish writers, such as Beckett and Flann O'Brien, and particularly Joyce in *Ulysses* and *Finnegans Wake*. Swift indulged in this wordplay in many of his lighter works, in his poems in particular, and he was even unable to keep it out of *Gulliver's Travels*.

During this period he wrote one of his most powerful poems, 'A Description of a Salamander', which was an attack on Lord Cutts, one of the Irish Lord Justices. He had heartily disliked Cutts for many years and in the poem he presents him as an impotent lecher trying to ply his trade in Ireland. Cutts, a soldier who had won fame in battle, had gained the nickname 'Salamander' (a type of lizard) for bravery under fire. Swift takes up the comparison and, taking liberties with the description of salamanders found in the natural history of the Roman writer Pliny, presents the creature as a serpent which is loathsome and produces a 'filthy froth', which in contact with the skin 'spreads leprosy and baldness round'. It is but a short step to suggesting that Cutts is

. . . a battered beau
By age and claps grown cold as snow. (I, 84)

It is an unfair poem since Cutts's only real fault was vanity, but it shows Swift at his most virulent, though perhaps here using too much power on too undeserving [34] a victim.

At the same time, in 1707, he was writing *The Story of the Injured Lady*, his first essay in the Irish cause, where he portrays Ireland as a woman who has been raped by England. The work is in the form of an allegory, a form which he had so successfully employed in *A Tale of a Tub*. The Lady (Ireland) has been ruined and cast off by a gentleman (England), who is now set to marry the Lady's rival (Scotland). The Lady feels particularly badly used because she is so much more attractive than her rival and because she has previously been so open and trusting towards the gentleman. Swift outlines Ireland's relations with England in terms of the allegory: for example, the lady was won 'half by force, and half by consent' (IX, 5), a description of Ireland's submission to Henry II. The gentleman is shortly to marry the rival (the Act of Union between England and Scotland). The Lady's friends advise her to call together her tenants (the Irish Parliament) and to pass resolutions which would make her less dependent on her former suitor. Swift did not have the pamphlet published in his lifetime, because its condemnation of England might have prejudiced the negotiations which the Church of Ireland was about to begin to obtain the remission of the First Fruits. The pamphlet is vital as an early statement of his position over what Ireland should do to alleviate her suffering: the duty of the Irish people, he says, is to take positive action. It also shows his familiarity with the work of William Molyneux, which formed the basis for the Drapier's position some years later.

In June 1706 a nephew of Sir William Temple had invited Swift to visit Moor Park: he replied:

I am extremely obliged by your kind invitation to

Moor Park, which no time will make me forget or love less. If I love Ireland better than I did, it is [35] because we are nearer related, for I am deeply allied to its poverty. My little revenue is sunk two parts in three, and the third in arrears. Therefore, if I come to Moor Park it must be on foot; but then comes another difficulty; that I carry double the flesh you saw about me at London; to which I have no manner of title, having neither purchased it by luxury nor good humour (i, 54-5).

However, little more than a year later he felt more financially stable, had become friendly with the new Lord Lieutenant, Lord Pembroke, and was asked by Archbishop King to be the official negotiator in London for the First Fruits. So in November 1707 he sailed for England as part of Pembroke's official entourage.

The Prince of Journalists

Swift was unsuccessful in the matter of the First Fruits and as a result, after months of negotiations with politicians, he must have felt very strongly the deviousness of politicians, which he later attacked in *Gulliver's Travels*. In fact, the English government did not intend to advise the Queen to remit the First Fruits unless the Irish church agreed to the repeal of the Test Act. So all his carefully laid plans were in ruins and his already shaky association with the Whigs was under increasing pressure.

But while in England at this time he made new friends. He became friendly with Addison, later the editor of *The Spectator*, who described him as 'the most agreeable companion, the truest friend, and the greatest genius of the age'. Addison introduced him to his friend Steele, whose *Tatler* initiated the literary journalism which played such an important part in eighteenth-century literature and politics. He also became friendly with the poet and diplomat Matthew Prior and with the poet Ambrose Phillips (the original 'Namby Pamby'). Addison was an important literary influence on Swift at this time, suggesting many revisions of his early poetic success 'Baucis and Philemon'. Swift collaborated with Steele over *The Tatler* and it was in this periodical that one of his few widely known poems, ' A Description of the Morning' appeared in 1709. It is a poem of eighteen lines presenting a vibrant portrait of the dawn chorus in grimy London (as opposed to the dawn choruses of so many contemporary pastoral [37] poems). The London dawn chorus has hackney coaches, a maid slipping from her master's bed, the 'slipshod prentice' sweeping outside his master's shop, the coal merchant shouting his wares, the chimney sweep, the turnkey at the prison watching the return of his 'flock', who have been let out for the night to steal the money for their board and lodging, and finally, schoolboys, who 'lag with satchels in their hands'. The contemporary reader would have seen that Swift was parodying the pastoral poem of the day by representing its figures in a very different landscape: for example, the turnkey is an echo of the shepherd, but of course has a very different relationship with *his* 'flock'.

During 1707—8 Swift wrote two prose works which are indicative of his general style. In *The Bickerstaff Papers* he took on the pseudonym of one Isaac Bickerstaff to pillory the fraudulent astrologer John Partridge who had been producing what must have been an eighteenth-century rival of *Old Moore's Almanac*. Partridge was a fervent defender of Dissenters and a supporter of occasional conformity and other measures which Swift opposed; he believed too that he could foretell deaths. Swift entered into Partridge-baiting with joy and predicted that 'Partridge the almanac-maker . . . will infallibly die upon the 29th of March next, about eleven at night of a raging fever' (II, 125). He wrote poems, such as 'An Elegy on Mr Patrige', as well as prose pieces, and was so effective that Partridge had virtually to *prove* his continued existence. As Bickerstaff, Swift was indulging in one of his favourite devices: takes on the identity of the target of his satire. He even made Bickerstaff an astrologer although there can be no doubt that he detested astrologers.

On a more serious note Swift wrote the *Argument*
[38] *against Abolishing Christianity*, which took up much
of his visit to London in 1708, when he was still in
league with the Whigs. This excellent example of his
irony was directed against deists and freethinkers,
and was so written that their followers would be sure
to read it, mistaking it for one of their own effusions.
In the pamphlet he envisages that plans have already
been drawn up for the abolition of Christianity. This
very exaggerated distortion of the Whig position was
seized on by the Tory Anglicans, who would believe
anything of their opponents.

The author of the pamphlet again occupies the
middle ground and Swift speaks from behind the
author's mask. In this case the author is a *persona*,
who intends to abolish the Christian religion but
needs to be convinced that the results will be beneficial. A number of arguments are presented in
favour of abolition and dealt with one by one. Some
of them are quite preposterous even though put
forward in an objective fashion: Christianity and its
members should be retained because they provide
targets for the wit and learning of freethinkers; an
extra day in the week would be gained; the clergy
could join the army and navy. But Swift's mask slips
occasionally and we can see his own contempt for
freethinkers. His techniques are clever and in fact
prefigure those used later in *Gulliver's Travels* and
A Modest Proposal. In the pamphlet, for example, he
uses exaggerations and plays with mathematics: 'It
is likewise urged, that there are, by computation, in
this kingdom, above ten thousand parsons whose
revenues . . . would suffice to maintain at least two
hundred young gentlemen of wit and pleasure . . .'
(II, 30). It is always difficult for Swift's readers to
be sure of his standpoint because his prose irony is
so intricate and double-edged. He is attacking unscrup-

ulous agnostics, who used Christianity as a social convenience, who favoured the Establishment of the [39] Church with the gospel omitted. Nominal Christianity, the author argues, should be retained — but for very unlikely reasons.

The pamphlet was perhaps more of a typical Swiftian *jeu d'esprit* than a serious contribution to political struggles, and although it was published in 1710 the Whigs had rather anticipated it by ordering a proposed Bill for the repeal of the Test Act to be burned by the common hangman, thus removing most of the fears of Church of England men that the Whigs were out to destroy the Church.

During the winter of 1708–9 Swift was in bad health. For one thing his labyrinthine vertigo, or Ménière's disease, was occurring more frequently and he was treating it quite uselessly with violent exercise and a lack of fruit. But when not suffering bouts of illness he displayed tremendous energy as he did for most of his life. He enjoyed walking, riding, swimming and rowing. He read feverishly, talked and played cards in taverns and clubs with friends and acquaintances and he despatched numerous letters. He once described his mind as 'a conjured spirit which would do mischief if he did not give it employment' (i, 4). This was the pattern of his whole life, whether at the centre of political life in London or in his country retreat at Laracor. Among his friends were a great many women, for he had an easy manner with women and was extremely popular with them. However, the greatest impact on him was made by Esther Vanhomrigh, whom he nicknamed 'Vanessa'. Her mother was the widow of a prosperous Dutch merchant who lived in Dublin, and Esther, the eldest of four children, was twenty-one years younger than Swift. When the widowed Mrs Vanhomrigh moved to London, Swift, who had probably known

the family in Dublin, became a frequent visitor and
Stella was at first quite suspicious. Vanessa was an extrovert person, who was in many ways Swift's equal, and although he acted the role of tutor (as he always did in his relationships with women) she was spirited enough to stand up to him. He had first met her at an inn at Dunstable and eventually he came to be treated as a member of the family in their Chelsea home. Although he tried to make her behave as discreetly as Stella always did this was not in her nature:

> There is not a better girl on earth. I have a mighty friendship for her. She has good principles, and I have corrected all her faults; but I cannot persuade her to read, though she has an understanding, memory and taste, that would bear great improvement. But she is incorrigibly idle and lazy — she thinks the world was made for nothing but perpetual pleasure . . . She makes me of so little consequence that it almost distracts me. She will bid her sister go downstairs before my face, for she has 'some private business with the Doctor' (i, 278).

Because they met frequently in London there is little correspondence between them. There has been much speculation about the relationship and it does seem that in this case there actually was a physical relationship (*3*, 148). But Swift eventually backed away, as he had done with Varina, when Vanessa became too persistent in Dublin.

The General Election of 1708 produced the most Whig-dominated Parliament since the Revolution and Swift realised that there was now no hope of any progress with the First Fruits. So in June 1709, after a visit to his mother, which turned out to be his last sight of her, he returned to Ireland somewhat dejected.

He then spent fourteen months in Ireland. In Dublin

he enjoyed the company of his friend Addison, who was there as Secretary to the detested Lord Lieutenant, [41] the Earl of Wharton. Swift saw a good deal of Addison but deliberately avoided Wharton whenever possible. As usual, he travelled round the country spending weeks with friends such as Charles Ford at Wood Park between Dublin and Laracor. He was also able to pursue his friendship with Stella. He improved his estate at Laracor, planting hedges and fruit trees and cutting the willows. In April 1710 his mother died and he wrote with affection of her virtues.

Back in England during 1709 Harley was working energetically to bring about the downfall of the Whig government. The English were growing tired of the protracted wars on the Continent and wanted an end to them. The Queen herself asked 'Will this bloodshed never cease?' and began to make changes in the government so that it was not to be long before the Tories would get their chance to rule. Wharton was anxious to get back to England and he left in August 1710 accompanied by Swift, who was once again empowered by the Irish bishops to try for the First Fruits.

2

Shortly after arriving in London Swift wrote 'I am perfectly resolved to return as soon as I have done my commission whether it succeeds or no. I ne'er went to England with so little desire in my life' (JS, I, 4). 'I protest upon my life, I am heartily weary of this town, and wish I had never stirred' (JS, I, 16). His view of London at the time can be seen in 'A Description of a City Shower', which appeared in *The Tatler*, and can be regarded as complementing his earlier 'Description of the Morning'.

The poem shows how ludicrous it would be to attempt [42] to deal with city life in the popular contemporary form of the pastoral poem. But, while Swift has much fun with his imitation of Virgil, the greatest of the classical pastoral poets (both in the form of the poem and in his treatment of various aspects of the street scene), he succeeds brilliantly in bringing home to the reader what it must have been like to live in London at the time. The poem shows a wild helter-skelter of activity, but he controls it all as the Shower sweeps away all the filth and chaos of the city and he builds up to a physically repulsive yet wholly realistic conclusion:

Sweepings from butchers' stalls, dung, guts and blood,
Drowned puppies, stinking sprats, all drenched in mud,
Dead cats and turnip-tops come tumbling down the flood (I, 139).

Swift called once again on Godolphin with very little expectation of success. The latter had just been dismissed from office as Lord Treasurer after a lifetime of service to Queen Anne and had been ordered to break his staff of office without even a farewell audience. 'I found my Lord Godolphin the worst dissembler of any of them that I have talked to,' Swift wrote (i, 177). He then decided to seek revenge, 'I have almost finished my lampoon, and will print it for revenge on a certain great person' (JS, I, 37). So he abbreviated Godolphin's Christian name to 'Sid', turned his staff of office into a 'rod' and elaborated on different kinds of rod. His fertile mind was employed to the full: Moses's rod used to strike the rock, the magician's wand, the witch's broomstick, a water-divining rod and so on. Godolphin is reduced not on this occasion to an animal (as happens in many of Swift's lampoons and satires) but to a pantomime figure of fun. His rod had once brought him wealth [43] and power but now Swift talks to him like a naughty child:

Dear Sid, then why wer't thou so mad
To break thy rod like naughty lad?
You should have kissed it in your distress,
And then returned it to your mistress,
Or made it a Newmarket switch,
And not a rod for thy own breech.
For since old Sid has broken this,
His next will be a rod in piss. (I, 135)

Swift began to see how useful he could be to politicians: ''Tis good to see what a lamentable confession the Whigs all make me of my ill usage; but I mind them not. I am already represented to Harley [the Tory leader] as a discontented person, that was ill used for not being Whig enough; and I hope for good usage from him. The Tories drily tell me I may make my fortune, if I please; but I do not understand them, or rather, I do understand them' (JS, I, 35-6). Swift was well received by Harley, who was much to his taste, being a well-read man, who could exchange quips, and who was, above all, a middle-of-the-road politician, which suited Swift's dislike of party extremists. Harley was immediately receptive to Swift's mission on behalf of the First Fruits, 'He heard me tell my business; entered into it with all kindness; asked me for my powers, and read them; and read likewise a memorial I had drawn up and put it in his pocket to show the Queen; told me the measures he would take, and in short, said everything I could wish: told me he must bring Mr St John and me acquainted; and spoke so many things of personal kindness and esteem for me that I am inclined half to believe . . . that he would do everything to bring me over' (JS, I, 45-6). Swift [44] never received the praise he deserved for his part in successfully obtaining the remission of the First Fruits for the Irish church. As late as 1716 he was himself applying for help for his own parish from the board set up to administer the fund and asked them for a clause to be inserted in the deed mentioning his own role in securing the remission. This was not granted.

Harley realised that Swift would be vital to the urgent propaganda exercise he needed to mount in order to gain office. It was later realised that Queen Anne's successor would be the Hanoverian George I, sympathetic to the Whigs. So Harley arranged for Swift to take over the *Examiner* and to write a weekly article for it. Swift's task was to present the political ideas given him by Harley or his lieutenant St John; for this he refused financial reward. *The Examiner* was, in true Swiftian style, anonymously edited, and he seems to have been able to write his 2,000 word essays in about seven days. He took over the editorship in October 1710 and his first issue appeared on Thursday 2 November. In all, he wrote thirty-two numbers and the last for which he was totally responsible appeared on 7 June 1711. So Swift left the Whigs — or rather, as he would have preferred to put it, they left him; his disenchantment with them centred on their ecclesiastical policy rather than on anything fundamentally anti-Whig in his general views. In fact, it can be said that although he was intellectually inclined to the Whigs his temperament took him to the side of the Tories, particularly when they were led by Harley and St John.

The general tenor of Swift's writing in the *Examiner* was that the Whigs were deficient in all virtues and therefore the opposite of the Tories. In all the numbers he achieved a superb appearance of consistency, even though he continued to contradict [45] himself (saying, for example, that he would avoid controversy and then involving himself in it; denouncing the epithets 'Whig' and 'Tory' and then using them himself). Week after week he kept up the onslaught on those opposed to the Ministry, and presented a dazzling display of political journalism hardly ever equalled since. He is one of the greatest journalists and propagandists in English; it is no surprise that the great political journalist and propagandist, Michael Foot, follows Cobbett and Orwell in enthusiastic support for Swift.

Swift used the *Examiner* in particular to attack Wharton and the Duke of Marlborough. The former, late Lord Lieutenant in Ireland, was a powerful Whig, who was closely linked with what Swift saw as the anti-church movement, while the latter represented the discredited Whig Ministry and the continuing war against France. As well as having political reasons for attacking the two men, Swift was also able to satisfy his innate urge to achieve creative satisfaction through lampooning individuals.

In the *Examiner* of 30 November 1710 he launched his fiercest attack on Wharton, making the analogy with Verres, the Roman governor of Sicily whom Cicero had attacked. As so often was the case with allegory and analogy the historical procedure gave perfect parallels for the satirist: 'I have brought here a man before you, my lords, who is a robber of the public treasure; an overturner of law and justice and the disgrace as well as destruction of the Sicilian province' (III, 27). Swift had never been friendly with Wharton and had once accused him of defecating on the high altar of Gloucester Cathedral. In December 1710 he produced the most severe of his attacks on Wharton, the *Short Character of his Excellency*

Thomas Earl of Wharton. Here he describes him as
[46] 'an ill dissembler and an ill liar, although they are the
two talents he most practises' (III, 179), and sums
him up: 'He is a presbyterian in politics, and an
atheist in religion; but he chooses at present to whore
with a papist' (III, 179).

The entire issue of 23 November 1710 was devoted
to Marlborough. Here again Swift used historical
parallels: it had cost the Romans £994.11.0 (including
2d for a crown of laurels) to honour a successful
general, whereas the cost of Marlborough's successes
to the grateful English public was £540,000. Swift
later used such financial and arithmetical ingenuity
in greater abundance in *A Modest Proposal* and *The
Drapier's Letters.*

3

Swift has left a vivid account of his life in London at
this time in his *Journal to Stella.* From this and from
his various account books and letters (there are five
volumes of his lively correspondence), we find that
his skill as an administrator and his very careful
husbandry (at times almost parsimony) made it
possible for him to live on a very small income.
Dr Johnson summed up his careful management:
'He was frugal by inclination, but liberal by principle,'[1] and elsewhere, 'At last his avarice grew too
powerful for his kindness; he would refuse a bottle
of wine, and in Ireland no man visits where he cannot
drink.'[2] The *Journal* reads very much like Pepys's
Diary in its attention to small but essential details of
everyday life in London:

Today at last I dined with Lord Mountrath and
carried Lord Mountjoy and Sir Andrew Fountaine
with me and was looking over them at ombre till

eleven this evening like a fool. They played running ombre half crowns, and Sir Andrew Fountaine won [47] eight guineas of Mr Coote; so I am come home late and will say but little to MD this night. I have gotten half a bushel of coals, and Patrick [Swift's servant], the extravagant whelp, had a fire ready for me; but I picked off the coals before I went to bed. It is a sign London is now an empty place when it will not furnish me with matter for above five or six lines in a day (JS, I, 51).

As he gradually changed his political allegiance it was inevitable that he would lose some friends. He managed to keep many, but not Addison, who was himself engaged in propaganda for the Whig side: 'Mr Addison and I hardly meet once a fortnight: his Parliament and my different friendships keep us asunder' (JS, I, 119). In October 1710 there was a Tory landslide victory and, largely on the basis of their promises of peace on the Continent, Harley and St John were returned to political power, which they exercised until the death of the Queen in 1714. These became Swift's great years at the centre of political power.

As he lost the friendship first of Addison and then of Steele, Swift became more and more important to the Tory rulers, who, it is important to note, sought his support, rather than he theirs. He was in a sense being used by the Tories but it is doubtful whether he knew this at the time; however, he was happy in the friendship of Harley and St John. Harley was some six years older than Swift and much like a father figure to him, while St John was eleven years younger, 'a young man with half the business of the nation upon him, and the applause of the whole,' wrote Swift of him (VIII, 135). In addition, he constantly linked St John with his beloved Sir

William Temple in appearance, attributes and accom-
plishments.

In March 1711 a middle-aged French emigré, the self-styled Marquis de Guiscard, attempted to murder Harley, and Swift reported the attempt to Archbishop King from the centre of events. Later that year Harley became Earl of Oxford and Lord Treasurer. At this time the Tories were proceeding cautiously to get rid of the Marlboroughs. Although the Duchess had been dismissed by the Queen and replaced as confidante by Harley's friend Mrs Masham, the Duke was still at the head of the allied armies. The two of them were busy building their magnificent palace at Blenheim and they had immeasurable wealth (Marlborough alone is reputed to have made £750,000 per annum in today's terms). Between November 1710 and June 1711 Swift worked conscientiously in the *Examiner* for Marlborough's downfall. Then Marlborough made the mistake of demanding that the Queen make him Captain General for life, a request which, if granted, would have made him virtually a dictator.

Swift continued the attack on Marlborough with his major political tract, *The Conduct of the Allies*, which was a statement of the government's case and was more partisan than anything he had previously written. There was a ferocious battle in the Lords when a combination of Whigs and 'Diehard' Tories carried a motion opposing a negotiated peace. Oxford, however, persuaded the Queen to create twelve new peers and with their votes the peace was carried. Shortly afterwards, Marlborough was dismissed from all his offices. *The Conduct of the Allies*, which appeared in November 1711, was a direct attack on him and a great success. In it Swift stated the government's case and presented in particular the views of St John. Everyone was tired of the war, 'Ten glorious campaigns are passed, and now at last, like the sick man, we are just expiring with all sorts of good [49] symptoms' (VI, 20). The pamphlet sold extremely well: the first edition of a thousand copies was sold out in two days and the next printing was gone in five hours. Eventually, six editions were published in two months, comprising 11,000 copies. Swift told Stella: 'The Tory lords and commons in Parliament argue all from it, and all agree, that never anything of that kind was of so great consequence, or made so many converts' (JS, II, 441). He presented the continental war as virtually a Marlborough family affair:

> ... what have we been fighting for all this while? The answer is ready; we have been fighting for the ruin of the public interest, and the advancement of a private. We have been fighting to raise the wealth and grandeur of a particular family, to enrich usurers and stock-jobbers, and to cultivate the pernicious designs of a faction, by destroying the landed interest. The nation begins now to think these blessings not worth fighting for any longer, and therefore desires a peace (VI, 59).

Swift never met the Marlboroughs as he never met the Queen, but like everyone else he knew of their love of money and power. His attack on Marlborough consisted, apart from *The Conduct of the Allies*, in three issues of *The Examiner* and several briefer pieces later, including 'The Fable of Midas', which attacked Marlborough's greed. In this poem he tells the traditional tale of Midas (who turned into gold everything he touched) but in a burlesque style which results in Midas's gift being derided:

> A codling e'er it went his lip in,
> Would straight become a golden pippin. (I, 156)

Having reduced the mythological Midas to a figure of [50] fun, Swift then invites his readers 'to think upon a certain leader' and the parallels between the events in the poem and Marlborough's life would have made this easy. Marlborough's greed for wealth and preferment is turned by Swift to something concrete:

> But gold defiles with frequent touch,
> There's nothing fouls the hands so much:
> And scholars give it for the cause,
> Of British Midas dirty paws. (I, 158)

At the end of the poem Marlborough stands discredited:

> And Midas now neglected stands,
> With ass's ears and dirty hands. (I, 158)

Looked back on, Swift's contribution to Marlborough's fall was significant but not particularly vicious. However, he did write a rather pointed 'Satirical Elegy on the Death of a Late Famous General' after Marlborough had died. This poem is a caricature, and therefore something of a distortion, of its subject. Swift seems anxious to use the example of Marlborough to teach a lesson for the future. He paid little attention to the traditional reverence for the dead and felt that men too powerful to be attacked while alive should be attacked after death because 'although their memories will rot, there may be some benefit for their survivors, to smell it while it is rotting' (XII, 25). He makes the traditional point that man must return to the earth whence he came, but unlike traditional elegies, Swift's is written in that conversational tone of which he was the master:

> His Grace! impossible! what dead!
> Of old age too, and in his bed! (I, 296)

His use of conversational language does much to

reduce to a proper perspective such godlike figures as Marlborough and it is not long before he suggests that [51] 'This world he cumbered long enough' and that he left behind 'so great a stink'. The bystanders are invited to approach the coffin and examine 'How very mean a thing's a Duke' and the poem concludes:

From all his ill-got honours flung,
Turned to that dirt from whence he sprung. (I, 297)

4

Still Swift failed to gain promotion. Although he succeeded in his friendship with Oxford and St John, he failed to make any progress with the Queen, who scarcely noticed him and, in fact, despite the efforts of Oxford, she never called on Swift to preach before her. It has always been thought that a chief reason for this indifference was her fervent dislike of *A Tale of a Tub*, which as a very devout Anglican she considered to be somewhat improper. It is also possible, since she was highly susceptible to the views of those around her, that she ignored Swift's friend Lady Masham and was influenced by the hatred for Swift felt by his enemy the red-haired Duchess of Somerset. Swift attacked the latter in a very witty and hostile poem, employing all his love of punning. He brought in the Duchess's family origins as daughter of the Earl of Northumberland; her second marriage to Thomas Thynne of Longleat; Thynne's rival Count Konigsmark, one of whose servants shot Thynne; and her third marriage to the Duke of Somerset:

Beware of carrots from Northumberland.
Carrots sown Thyn a deep root may get,
If so be they are in Somer set:
Their connings Mark thou, for I have been told
They assassin when young and poison when old.

Root out these carrots, O thou whose name
Is backwards and forwards always the same;

[Masham]

And keep close to thee always that name
Which backwards and forwards is almost the same

[Anne]

And England, wouldst thou be happy still,
Bury those carrots under a Hill.   [Lady Masham
née Hill] (I, 148)

Swift did not increase his chances with the Queen by publishing this poem, 'The Windsor Prophecy', in 1711 against the advice of Lady Masham. Three years later he wrote of the Duchess's ferocious response to his attack:

Now Madam Coningsmark her vengeance vows
On Swift's reproaches for her murdered spouse,
From her red locks her mouth with venom fills:
And thence into the Royal ear instills. (I, 195)

He continued to move in the highest political and court circles and St John got him into The Society, an influential social club set up in opposition to the Whig Kit-Cat Club. In addition, he became friendly at Windsor with Dr John Arbuthnot, who later became an important friend to Pope as well as a member of the Scriblerus Club.

After 1711 Swift experienced a burst of creative activity. He proposed to Harley the formation of 'a society or academy for correcting and settling our language, that we may not perpetually be changing as we do' (JS, I 295). *A Proposal for Correcting, Improving, and Ascertaining the English Tongue* was published on 17 May 1712 and for the first time Swift's name appeared at the end of his work. The idea of such an academy made up of paid men of letters, who would reform and purify the English language, was prevalent in England even before the foundation of the French Academy in 1635. The idea is in conformity with Swift's general conservatism, [53] since he felt that the English language was becoming corrupted by misuse. He begins the pamphlet with a review of the language in which he tries to show that English has suffered from influences such as military invasions and corruptions from the French. With hindsight we can see that his scholarship was faulty. He admits that change is necessary for a language but argues that endless, rapid change is not necessary, attacking in particular new words, contractions, slang and other innovations. He then presents a scheme for reform, which would involve the appointment of persons qualified to judge questions of language. These men should regularise grammar, condemn errors, banish certain words, correct others and bring back lost usages. Finally, he deals with the benefits likely to ensue from the scheme, chief among which would be the preservation of literary works.

It might seem strange that Swift did not side with Johnson in rejecting the idea of an academy since he was himself such a manipulator of language. However, the linguistic conservatism which he expresses here is only another facet of the concern he expressed for the stability of Britain's political constitution. He regarded all man-made achievements as unlikely to last and so constantly in need of re-statement. At the time he wrote the pamphlet the Dissenters were threatening the established church, the Whigs were a political threat and dunces and pedants, he thought, were ruining the language; so he felt the need to stand firm. Swift himself always wrote in a style which was plain and clear. It is well known that he read his poetry to his servants and made any changes necessary for their understanding. In 1712, in 'A Letter to a Young Gentleman lately entered into Holy

Orders', he gave practical advice on preaching and [54] advocated simple unaffected language free from cliché.

In 1712 Bolingbroke (St John had been created a Viscount) brought in the Stamp Act, which taxed newspapers and pamphlets and proposed that the author's name should appear on all his writings (a proposal subsequently defeated). Swift produced more than seven pamphlets in the few days before the Act came into force on 1 August.

In the meantime he continued his daily routine in London and recorded everything in his *Journal to Stella*. He lived with his habitually drunk Irish servant Patrick, who caused him a good deal of trouble:

> We have plays acted in our town, and Patrick was at one of them, oh ho. He waa damably mauled one day when he was drunk; he was at cuffs with a brother footman, who dragged him along the floor upon his face, which looked for a week after as if he had the leprosy; and I was glad enough to see it. I have been ten times sending him over to you; yet now he has new clothes and a laced hat' (JS, I, 302).

By 1712 Swift was able to pick and choose whom he visited or dined with. He particularly frequented the homes of Oxford, where he dined two or three times a week with Bolingbroke, Lady Masham, Lady Orkney or the Ormondes. But Oxford and Bolingbroke kept from him the fact that they were in touch with the Stuart Pretender in France and he was totally taken in by them.

In 1712 he began work on *The History of the Four Last Years of the Queen*, which was to be an account of how the Tories had achieved the peace in Europe. He had always wanted to be an historian and at the time his hopes for preferment were so high that he actually aspired to become Historiographer Royal. [55] This account, unfortunately, which he felt was to be as important as his other political writings, did not appear until after his death in 1758: he ran into considerable difficulties and found it impossible to obtain all the necessary help from the Ministry, some people thought the work too dangerous to publish and Sir Thomas Hanmer, to whom Swift lent the manuscript, kept it for three months. By the time the work was completed in the middle of May 1713 the occasion for which it was being prepared had passed, as Parliament had obtained the Queen's formal announcement of peace. The work concentrates on the events of only sixteen months and does so dramatically rather than historically, since it turns the history into the drama of the performers involved. In the *Conduct* Swift had been able to expose the faults of his political enemies; here he had to write with considerable tact since he was seeking to justify the actions of his own side. The book reveals his gullibility in believing everything politicians had told him, but it also anticipates certain of his views, such as those on population, which would be used in later works. The best features of the book are the characters drawn of the leading personalities. Marlborough is accused of avarice and cowardice, megalomania and hypocrisy, treachery and barbarism, while he writes of Sunderland, 'It seems to have been this gentleman's fortune to have learned his divinity from his father, and his politics from his tutors' (VII, 9).

Suddenly in 1713 good news came Swift's way. He was unlikely to obtain an Irish bishopric, which would have needed the consent of the Queen, but he was given the deanery of St Patrick's Cathedral when the former dean was promoted to a bishopric.

He landed in Dublin in June and was installed in St
[56] Patrick's on 13 June. Archbishop King summed up
the promotion: 'a Dean could do less mischief than a
bishop'.

5

Swift had seen a great deal of the Vanhomrighs while
in London and been involved in secret meetings with
Vanessa. She wrote him pressing letters in the summer
of 1713 and he seems to have been embarrassed, but
unwilling to end the relationship. This was a character-
istic which he displayed throughout his life (since he
was equally unable to end his relationship with his
patron Temple). He had encouraged Vanessa to
develop her critical powers and to become increasingly
reliant on him as mentor. He had cut her off from
her old world and yet did not provide security for
her in his own. It is not surprising that she later
wrote to him in despair. He continued, however,
to develop his relationships with both Vanessa and
Stella and each was able to give him different satis-
factions which he needed. Nigel Dennis points out
that whereas Swift's relationship with Stella on the
one hand and Vanessa on the other is similar to the
familiar story of Pygmalion and Galatea, in the Irish
version (as told later by Bernard Shaw) the inspired
image falls in love with its creator.[3] What women
received from Swift, Dennis suggests, was *attention*,
and men like Swift are never husbands (but more
likely priests, celibates and teachers).

In the autumn he sought refuge in verse and wrote
a poetic account of the affair, which he called
'Cadenus and Vanessa' ('Cadenus' being an anagram
of 'Decanus', the Latin for 'Dean'). The poem was
intended for Vanessa and not for publication, but
was found among her papers after her death and

published in 1726. In the poem he suggests that Vanessa was not lacking in beauty and seductive [57] powers but that Cadenus was incapable of returning her love. If the poem does indeed set out his attitude to Vanessa then he was clearly trying to keep her at arm's length. The poem describes a beautiful girl, endowed by the gods with intelligence and virtue and rising far above the inadequate men and silly women she met in her society. She meets Cadenus, twice her age but 'grown old in politics and wit', who becomes her teacher and moral guide. But he cannot reciprocate her love:

> Cadenus, common forms apart,
> In every scene had kept his heart;
> Had sighed and languished, vowed and writ,
> For pastime or to show his wit;
> But time and books and state affairs
> Had spoiled his fashionable airs;
> He now could praise, esteem, approve,
> But understood not what was love. (II, 703)

He can return only friendship for passion.

The whole action of the poem takes place in a mythological framework where Vanessa has been sent by Venus, as an experiment, to resolve a lawsuit in the court of love. The poem can be seen as central to Swift's major preoccupations in that he makes women representatives of that aspect in human relationships which distracts men from what is rational; but men are just as much to blame for allowing themselves to be put in such positions. His portrayal of himself as the comic, unemotional, shy Cadenus is an amusing one (for example, he is physically struck by an arrow from Cupid), but behind the humorous exterior of the poem lies the sad theme that a true and intelligent relationship between the sexes is in his view virtually impossible.

But Swift, as so often, keeps the reader at bay, hiding
[58] his own true feelings in the awkward rhymes and rhythms of the poem and in the refusal to be serious for long. He is using verse, as he so often used the mask in prose, to avoid too close a personal involvement. Swift never lets us get close to him. In his prose he wrote in the persons of other people, in the poetry he usually refused to be serious for long. The nearest we ever come to him is in his letters, but even there one feels he so often puts up a smokescreen of banter, raillery and exaggeration.

A good deal of critical energy has been directed to the problem of Swift's own psychological state. Ehrenpreis suggests that this poem is an indication of his attitudes arising from his father's death soon after his conception: 'The view of love as destructive and shortlived, of friendship as rational and enduring' (2, 649). He continues by suggesting that Swift's memories of boyhood when his mother and sister lived far away from him led to 'the view of desirable women as goddesses who seldom walk here below' (2, 649). In addition, he argues that the inconclusiveness of the central episode of the poem suggests the ambivalence of a man who had never been able to live either with women or without them. Swift received from Vanessa only part of the satisfaction he searched for in his relationships with women; Stella was the complement to Vanessa. He always produced reasons for not marrying: his own age, the age of the woman, his lack of money. But it is also possible to cite his diffidence, his hyper-sensitiveness, and we must consider that very important inner dependence he always exhibited, which led him to seek solitude. In addition, he may have had quite genuine reluctance to marry, not least because of his fear of insanity and because he feared he might not be able to bring to marriage a total commitment.

Swift sailed from Ireland on 29 August 1713 for his last significant stay in England. He had officially [59] stopped writing regularly for the *Examiner* in the summer of 1711 but continued to help from time to time. A rift had developed between Oxford and Bolingbroke and the former was gradually losing his hold on political office and had now lost the confidence of the Queen. Swift was torn between the two men, being devoted to Oxford's character but leaning towards Bolingbroke's policies. Later he wrote to Oxford: 'In your public capacity you have often angered me to the heart, but as a private man never once (ii, 44).

The main consolation for Swift at this time was the formation of the Scriblerus Club, which met in early 1714, and consisted of Swift, John Gay the poet, Dr Arbuthnot, Thomas Parnell, an Irish poet living in London, and Alexander Pope, with whom by this stage Swift had struck up what was to become a life-long friendship; Oxford was an honoured guest.

The Queen had been seriously ill in December 1713 and it became obvious to Swift that the rule of his friends and his own fortunes would only last as long as she lived. With a feeling of gloom he retreated to his friend John Geree's vicarage at Letcombe Bassett, three miles from Wantage in Berkshire. He managed some writing there but over everything was the sense of impending doom as everyone waited for the death of the Queen and the fall of Oxford.

At the beginning of August 1714 Vanessa arrived at Letcombe. 'You should not have come by Wantage for a thousand pound,' said Swift, angry at any hint of indiscretion, 'You used to brag you were very discreet; where is it gone?' (ii, 123). He then wrote to her, having made up his mind by this stage to leave for Ireland:

When I am there I will write to you as soon as I [60] can conveniently, but it shall be always under a cover; and if you write to me let some other direct it, and I beg you will write nothing that is particular, but what may be seen, for I apprehend letters will be opened and inconveniencies will happen. If you are in Ireland while I am there I shall see you very seldom. It is not a place for any freedom, but where everything is known in a week and magnified a hundred degrees. These are rigorous laws that must be passed through; but it is probable we may meet in London in winter, or if not, leave all to fate that seldom cares to humour our inclinations (ii, 123).

On 1 August the Queen died and Swift planned to leave for Ireland the next day. Oxford and Bolingbroke hung on to office for a while, but soon it became clear that their fall was imminent and Swift crossed to Dublin towards the end of August. Ironically, he discovered later that Bolingbroke had intended to reconcile him with the Duchess of Somerset and to secure his promotion to an English church post.

The Hibernian Patriot

1

Swift arrived in Dublin to take the oath to the new
king, George I. In fact, he virtually retired for a while
to the deanery. He was determined, he said, to 'grow
as stupid as the present situation of affairs will
require' (ii, 130). His party was out of office, the
Whigs had taken over, Archbishop King was in power
as a Lord Justice. He wrote to his friend Ford, 'I
expect the worst they can compass, and that they will
be able to compass it . . . I stay here to forget England
and make this place supportable by practice, and
because I doubt whether the present government
will give me a licence' (ii, 131-2). He also told Ford,
'I hope I shall keep my resolution of never meddling
with Irish politics' (a resolution he kept for only six
years) (ii, 127). He was extremely unhappy. His
friends were few in Ireland: Archdeacon Walls, Dr
Raymond of Trim and his vicar Worrall and curate
Warburton. Archbishop King suspected Swift because
of his close contacts with the Tories and their
relationship did not improve until the common cause
of Ireland brought them together. Of course Stella
and Mrs Dingley were there, but so was Vanessa, who
pursued him to Dublin, taking lodgings near Trinity
College in addition to her country house at Celbridge
outside Dublin. He spent some time avoiding Vanessa
because of the dangers of scandal: 'I will see you
tomorrow if possibly, you know it is not above five
days since I saw you, and I would ten times more if it

were at all convenient' (ii, 147). Vanessa pursued him
[62] further:

> Once I had a friend that would see me sometimes,
> and either commend what I did or advise me what
> to do, which banished all my uneasiness. But now,
> when my misfortunes are increased by being in a
> disagreeable place, amongst prying, deceitful
> people . . . you fly me, and give me no reason
> but that we are amongst fools and must submit . . .
> You once had a maxim, which was to act what
> was right and not mind what they [the world]
> said. I wish you would keep to it now. Pray what
> can be wrong in seeing and advising an unhappy
> young woman? . . . You can't but know that your
> frowns make my life insupportable. You have
> taught me to distinguish, and then you leave me
> miserable (ii, 148-9).

In addition to all this, he fell ill and wrote 'In Sickness'. This gloomy poem is subtitled 'written soon
after the Author's coming to live in Ireland, upon
the Queen's Death':

> But no obliging tender friend
> To help at my approaching end,
> My life is now a burthen grown
> To others, e'er it be my own. (I, 204)

The Dublin political scene after 1714 was over-
whelmingly Whig. The Lord Lieutenant, the Earl of
Sunderland, was a Whig, and four Whig members
of the Bar were given top posts: Alan Brodrick as
Chancellor, John Forster as Chief Justice of the
Court of Common Pleas, William Whitshed as Chief
Justice of the King's Bench and Joseph Deane as
Chief Baron of the Exchequor. A year after he had
been back in Ireland Swift wrote to Pope:

> You are to understand that I live in the corner of a

vast unfurnished house. My family consists of a steward, a groom, a helper in the stable, a footman, [63] and an old maid, who are all at board wages, and when I do not dine abroad, or make an entertainment (which last is very rare) I eat a mutton pie and drink half a pint of wine. My amusements are defending my small dominions against the Archbishop and endeavouring to reduce my rebellious choir (ii, 177).

The first Jacobite Rising took place in 1715 and Swift was in some danger since his Tory friends were thought to be in league with the exiled Stuart supporters and there were alarms everywhere. His friends Oxford and Bolingbroke actually went abroad to join the Pretender and Oxford was subsequently sent to the Tower of London. Swift's mail was opened, he was interrogated by Archbishop King and he was even hissed in the streets. The Commons voted for the impeachment of Oxford, Bolingbroke and Ormonde, and a letter from Ormonde to Swift was intercepted, as a result of which there was talk of keeping him in close confinement. He was being hounded by the Whigs both in Ireland and England.

Nevertheless, he made a number of friends in these early years and visited them in his travelling round Ireland. There was Knightley Chetwode, a Tory gentleman, who had two homes: one at Martry just north of Laracor, and the other at Woodbroke in the Queen's County. Then there were the Grattans of Belcamp: the eldest of the seven sons was later grandfather of the Irish patriot Henry Grattan. Swift also became friendly with the Rochforts of Gaulstown.

Some time during 1716 he is popularly supposed to have gone through a form of secret marriage with Stella in the garden of Bishop Ashe's house at Clogher. His early biographers agree that he insisted on com-

plete secrecy and that relations afterwards should be
[64] as they had been before the ceremony (3, 151-173),
but other biographers equally reject the marriage.
In Stella's will, which she signed, she is referred to
as 'spinster', and, in addition, Mrs Dingley, Mrs
Brent (Swift's housekeeper) and Dr Lyon (one of his
guardians at the end) all denied it.

At this time relations with Vanessa continued but
there was a five-year gap with only a single letter
from Swift. It is thought that letters were unnecessary
since they met frequently in Dublin. We know that
Vanessa was obsessed with Swift and that she marked
each of his visits to Celbridge by planting a laurel;
the gardener's boy there, when an old man, claimed
that she had been happy only when Swift visited her.
Se wrote him very sad letters, often full of increasing
passion and even desperation, but he replied as always:
drawing her to him and then appearing to repulse
her. He preferred to continue a relationship of raillery
and teasing. He wrote, 'If you write as you do, I shall
come the seldomer on purpose to be pleased with
your letters, which I never look into without wonder-
ing how a brat, who cannot read, can possibly write
so well' (ii, 235-6). Later that year (1720) she wrote
with some passion:

> Believe me, it is with the utmost regret that I now
> complain to you because I know your good nature
> such that you cannot see any human creature
> miserable without being sensibly touched. Yet
> what can I do? I must either unload my heart
> and tell you all its griefs or sink under the un-
> expressable distress I now suffer by your pro-
> digious neglect of me ... nor is the love I bear
> you only seated in my soul, for there is not a
> single atom of my frame that is not blended with
> it ... and my heart is at once pierced with sorrow

and love . . . If you have the least remains of pity for me left tell me tenderly. No, don't tell it so [65] that it may cause my present death and don't suffer me to live a life like a languishing death, which is the only life I can lead if you have lost any of your tenderness for me.

Vanessa died on 2 June 1723. Her death was not much commented on at the time. She had done much to disturb Swift's desire for a quiet life since she is said to have written to Stella to ask if the rumour of the marriage were true. Stella is said to have sent the letter to Swift and to have left Dublin without seeing him, whereupon he went to Celbridge, flung the letter down in front of Vanessa and left without a word. On her deathbed it is said that she refused to see a priest since it could not be Swift. She was buried in the old round church of St Andrew, which was burnt down in 1860 and her grave lost and forgotten. On her death Swift went on a 500-mile journey round Ireland.

For the next three or four years Swift's life continued in domestic vein with church business to occupy him and with visits to friends round Ireland. In 1718 he made friends with two young men with whom he was able to exchange witticism and linguistic jokes. One was Thomas Sheridan, a schoolmaster (the grandfather of the playwright, Richard Brinsley Sheridan) and the other was Patrick Delany, a Junior Fellow of Trinity College. Both were clergymen, and Swift, playing his usual role of father figure, was able to help them to promotion even though this was denied to him.

So he continued to live in this quiet way, writing little except light verse of a social nature. His ear trouble continued, 'I have the noise of seven watermills in my ears, and expect to continue so above a month . . . I mope at home, and can bear no company but trebles and counter-tenors' (iii, 36-7). Gradually he learnt to coexist with Archbishop King. The latter suffered from gout and Swift wrote to him: 'I own my head and your Grace's feet would be ill joined, but give me your head and take my feet, and match us in the kingdom if you can' (ii, 406).

Eventually, Swift accustomed himself to living in Ireland and to a very different manner of living from the hurly-burly of political life in London. During these years he did not become closely identified with any specifically Irish issues, secretly hoping that the political situation would change and that he could return to play a significant part in English public life again. He seems not to have enjoyed what he saw as a temporary residence in Ireland, which he called 'the most miserable country upon earth', and his writing in the first six years in Ireland was chiefly confined to poems of escapism and playful fun at the expense of friends.

During these years in exile he also wrote the first of his birthday poems to Stella as well as the first of his 'scatological' poems (which were later so much criticised for their alleged obscenity). In the group of eleven 'Birthday poems', which he wrote to Stella between 1719 and 1729 (mostly, but not always on her birthday) he examined a more positive side of that relationship between body and soul which he dissected in the scatological poems. Of all his poems these to Stella are the nearest he came to expressing his feelings directly rather than speaking through other voices. Stella's birthday was on 13 March and Swift wrote each year except 1726. The poems are birthday poems in name only and the ideas which they discuss mainly concern ageing and friendship. As we have seen, the friendship between Swift and Stella was a long and happy one and Yeats makes the poem Stella wrote to Swift the 'Words upon the

Window-pane' in his play of the same name:

> You taught how I might youth prolong
> By knowing what is right and wrong;
> How from my heart to bring supplies
> Of lustre to my fading eyes;
> How soon a beauteous mind repairs
> The loss of changed or falling hairs;
> How wit and virtue from within
> Can spread a smoothness o'er the skin.[1]

What is interesting about the poems is that they show a view of women not especially common at the time: a view in which women were seen as intelligent, sensitive, emancipated, equal and the friends of men. This is a view rather different from that of most early eighteenth-century poets.

Swift does not formulate his *feelings* for Stella, but addresses her in the same easy tone he uses to Pope, Arbuthnot and other friends, and equally he dwells on her spiritual virtues:

> Thou Stella, were no longer young,
> When first for thee my harp I strung:
> Without one word of Cupid's darts,
> Of killing eyes, or bleeding hearts:
> With friendship and esteem possesst,
> I ne'er admitted love a guest. (II, 728)

Despite the serious underlying intent of the poems he is often his habitual light-hearted, debunking self, using outrageous rhymes, making fun of the gods and goddesses and burlesquing the whole panoply of traditional poetic devices such as the Muse, the sublime and the inspiration claimed so pimpously by so many poets. In addition, this group of poems reinforces the point that his concerns were much the same in prose and poetry. It often seems that while the prose is the heavy artillery, the poems are his light skirmishing cavalry. In these poems, for example, he [68] is concerned with the illusion of permanence: Stella's virtues are constants in a world of change while her body (as his own) will grow old and die:

> No length of time can make you quit
> Honour and virtue, sense and wit,
> Thus you may still be young to me,
> While I can better hear than see;
> Oh, ne'er may fortune shew her spite,
> To make me deaf, and mend my sight. (II, 758)

We can compare the treatment of the same ideas in Books III and IV of *Gulliver's Travels*. Here Swift anticipates Yeats's 'After Long Silence':

> Bodily decrepitude is wisdom; young
> We loved each other and were ignorant.[2]

His whole life was devoted to a search for permanent values. He failed to find anything that was not transient, except perhaps his friendship with Stella. Physical beauty was particularly temporary and he makes this very clear in these birthday poems, even more vividly in the scatological poems and in comparable episodes in *Gulliver's Travels*. Pride taught men to think they could obtain some kind of permanence in life and he attacked pride at every turn.

2

In 1720 there was an awakening of Swift's old powers and the 'condition of Ireland' question brought him back to the centre of the public stage in a new role as an Irish patriot. It is true that as early as 1707, in *The Story of the Injured Lady*, he had expressed the grievance of the Irish clerical establishment against exploitation by the English, but his activity on that occasion had been chiefly on behalf of the Irish church and not as a spokesman for 'the [69] whole people of Ireland', which he became in 1724, when he created the figure of 'M.B., Drapier, saviour of his people'. Of course, since *The Story of the Injured Lady* was not published until after his death it was not a *public* statement of his views on Irish public affairs.

There has been much discussion about the extent of Swift's patriotism. In a letter to Pope in 1737 he even denied being Irish. The index to the *Correspondence* shows over eighty adverse or critical and only six approving comments about 'this miserable country', 'this vile country'. It is certainly easy to collect a series of exasperated outbursts about Ireland; at one time he saw Ireland as 'a madhouse'. However, a closer examination of these entries shows a gradual softening of his approach and a movement from a general condemnation of the country and its people to a wholesale attack on England for causing all the wretchedness. Some critics argue that in championing the Irish cause in *The Drapier's Letters* and other Irish tracts Swift was merely defending the constitutional rights of only one section of those who lived in Ireland, and in addressing 'the whole pople of Ireland' he had in mind only the Anglo-Irish. Certainly we can call him an 'Anglo-Irishman', with all the connotations of the term, especially what has been called the 'dilemma of identification'. In the twelfth century Maurice FitzGerald had spoken for the Anglo-Irish when he said, 'While we are English to the Irish we are Irish to the English.' Dr Johnson was in no doubt about what Swift did for Ireland: 'He taught them first to know their own interest, their weight, and their strength, and gave them spirit to assert that equality with their fellow-subjects to which they have ever since been making vigorous advances, and to claim those rights which they have [70] at last established. Nor can they be charged with ingratitude to their benefactor; for they reverenced him as a guardian, and obeyed him as a dictator.'[3] Whatever the view we take, in the end it was the people of Ireland who passed the final judgment on Swift's Irishness. For some years after the Drapier's victory in the matter of minting Irish coins in England, bonfires were lit in the streets of Dublin in celebration. Henry Grattan invoked the spirit of Swift in 1782, when the Irish parliament won its legislative independence: taking the floor of the Irish House of Commons, he said 'Spirit of Swift! Spirit of Molyneux! your genius has prevailed!' Michael Davitt, the nineteenth-century patriot, saw him, in Michael Foot's words, as 'the prophet of the land war and the supremacy of moral force' (*38*, 224). The Nationalist leader in Westminster, John Redmond, said in 1890 that Swift 'did as much as any man in history to lift Ireland into the position of a nation' (*38*, 224). W.B. Yeats was in no doubt about Swift's nationalism, 'Swift found his nationality through the *Drapier's Letters*, his convictions came from action and passion.'[4]

It is important to remember the relationship between England and Ireland up to Swift's time. England had consistently kept Ireland in the position of a subservient colonial power and the relationship between the two countries was summed up later in the eighteenth century when Edmund Burke said it was 'a machine of wise and elaborate contrivance, and as well fitted for the oppression, impoverishment, and degradation of a people, and the debasement, in them, of human nature itself, as ever proceeded from the perverted ingenuity of man'.[5] More recently, an economic historian has described Ireland in the eighteenth century as having 'all the disadvantages of both a colony and a foreign country without any of the advantages of either' (5, 25). The succession of intimidating laws passed by the London government had begun with the Navigation Act of 1663, which prohibited the export of goods to any English colony unless they were loaded in English ships at English ports. This did not immediately affect Ireland because horses and provisions from Ireland were excepted from the ban, and at the time Ireland had hardly any manufactured goods to export. But the Act treated Ireland as a colony and this was reinforced by the Navigation Acts of Charles II's reign, which were specifically aimed at Ireland. The import of Irish livestock into England, as well as butter and cheeses, followed, and the manufacture of wool took the place of livestock as Ireland's chief export trade. English mercantile interests next tried to strangle the woollen trade and the oppressive Woollen Act was passed in 1699. This prohibited the Irish from exporting their manufactured wool to any other country and allowed the export of unworked wool to only a few specified English ports under conditions which gave England a virtual monopoly in Irish raw wool. During the debate on the Act, one English M.P. stated quite openly that Ireland had to be humbled.

While the English Parliament was legislating to control Irish economic affairs there were Irishmen prepared to speak out. Sir William Petty had argued that Ireland hardly needed to import any goods from England, and the influential *The Case of Ireland's being bound by Acts of Parliament in England* was published by William Molyneux in 1698. This was reprinted many times in the eighteenth century and in it Molyneux maintained that the Irish Parliament had the right to legislate for Ireland: 'That Ireland should be bound by Acts of Parliament made in

England, is against reason and the common right of [72] all mankind'. He dwelt on Ireland's constitutional independence, condemned the appointment of Englishmen to Irish posts (which was widespread at the time) and reasserted Ireland's right to commercial freedom. The Irish government was a body without powers but it gave the illusion of some independence to Irish Protestants, though it did not meet at all between November 1715 and September 1723. Its Commons was seldom elected and usually met only once every two years to vote supplies, while a fifteenth-century statute had allowed the Dublin government to pass only laws which had previously been agreed by the Privy Council in London.

From the time he first arrived at St Patrick's Cathedral, Swift had noticed the poverty surrounding it and the poor economic state of the country. In 1715 he wrote 'I hear they think me a smart Dean and that I am for doing good. My motion is, that if a man cannot mend the public he should mend old shoes if he can do no better; and therefore I endeavour in the little sphere I am placed to do all the good it is capable of' (ii, 154). In a letter to his friend Ford in December 1719 he had hinted that his period of political inactivity was over, 'As the world is now turned, no cloister is retired enough to keep politics out' (ii, 330). He took no direct action over Irish affairs until he published his pamphlet *A Proposal for the Universal Use of Irish Manufacture* in 1720 (probably in May), which showed that he had an excellent grasp of the arguments already employed by Molyneux and that he knew of the disastrous effects on Irish trade of English punitive legislation.

As with so much of Swift's writing, an actual occasion prompted action: in 1720 it was the passing of the Declaratory Act by the English Parliament which caused him to write this pamphlet. The Act stated that 'the said kingdom of Ireland, hath been, [73] is, and of right ought to be subordinated unto and dependent upon the imperial crown of Great Britain . . .' (X, xviii, n4). Swift had other reasons for becoming involved in Irish affairs in that year. He was certainly not motivated in the first instance by any obvious patriotism or concern over Ireland's subject position in regard to England (a relationship much discussed in *The Drapier's Letters* and portrayed in Book Three of *Gulliver's Travels*, which he had interrupted in order to write the *Letters*). He realised that he would be able to attack old enemies (chiefly the Prime Minister Walpole) and pay off old scores, but there was now a new dimension brought to his political perspective. His life around St Patrick's Cathedral brought him into daily contact with the abject poverty of both Catholics and Protestants and he could clearly see that this poverty was the result of England's calculated exploitation of Ireland. He also felt that part of Ireland's sorry state was due to the factiousness, apathy and inability to act which so exasperated him. Throughout his life he worked equally for Catholics and Protestants, but at this time a severe depression had hit the mostly Protestant weavers (many of whom lived in the immediate vicinity of St Patrick's Cathedral), leading to considerable unemployment and even starvation. His spiritual leader, Archbishop King of Dublin, described the problem sympathetically and he was quick to follow. In addition, he was also aware of contemporary arguments about the claim of the English Parliament to legislate for Ireland and of the controversy over the emasculated powers of the Irish House of Lords when it came to passing laws.

The pamphlet was a natural successor to those of

Molyneux and others and Swift continued to raise [74] the constitutional issue of how far the Irish were obliged to be bound without their own agreement. The very title was calculated to infuriate the English authorities since it concluded with the words 'utterly rejecting and renouncing everything wearable that comes from England' (IX, 13). It was also an aggressive summary of the evils created by the laws passed against Irish manufacture and agriculture. In it he completely rejects and renounces everything that came from England (and he is said to have urged the Irish 'to burn everything from England except their people and their coals').

The pamphlet was printed in Dublin shortly before the celebrations arranged for the King's sixtieth birthday. It was immediately declared 'false, scandalous and seditious' and its printer prosecuted. Swift wrote an account of what had happened in a letter to Pope dated a few months after the pamphlet was published:

> This treatise soon spread very fast, being agreeable to the sentiments of the whole nation, except those gentlemen who had employments or were expectants. Upon which a person in great office here immediately took the alarm; he sent in haste for the Chief Justice and informed him of a seditious, factious and virulent pamphlet, lately published with a design of setting the two kingdoms at variance . . . The printer was seized, and forced to give great bail. After his trial the jury brought him in Not Guilty, although they had been culled with the utmost industry. The Great Justice sent them back nine times and kept them eleven hours until being perfectly tired out they were forced to leave the matter to the mercy of the judge by what they call a special verdict (ii, 367-8).

After a lengthy delay the Lord Lieutenant granted a writ of 'noli prosequi' and the case was dropped. But [75] now Swift was no longer seen by the Irish as a supicious alien (since everyone knew he was the author of the pamphlet) and he retaliated against the Grand Jury in the trial with his poem 'An Excellent New Song on a Seditious Pamphlet':

> Therefore I assure ye,
> Our noble Grand Jury,
> When they saw the Dean's book they were in a
> great fury:
> They would buy English silks for their wives
> and their daughters,
> In spite of his Deanship and journeyman Waters.
>
> (I, 237)

Swift failed, however, to achieve anything tangible with the pamphlet because what he proposed for Ireland needed far more active organisation than the Irish were in a position to offer.

About the same time that he was publishing the pamphlet a scheme was published in Ireland for creating a national bank similar to the Whigs' Bank of England. The South Sea Bubble madness was then at its height in England leading to the 'bursting of the bubble' in August and heavy financial losses for those who had dabbled. On 27 July 1721 a charter for a bank was granted, subject to Irish parliamentary approval, and Parliament, when it convened in September, looked favourably on the scheme but debated it vigorously for two months. Swift was opposed to the moneyed interest, seeing the whole business as a further intrusion by England into Irish affairs. The project was defeated in December and Swift commented to Archbishop King with whom he was united in opposition: 'I hear you are likely to be the sole opposer of the

Bank . . . bankrupts are always for setting up banks.
[76] How then can you think a bank will fail of a majority
in both Houses?' His ballad poem 'The Bank thrown
down' was an amusing display of punning:

> Pray what is this Bank of which the Town rings?
> The banks of a river I know are good things,
> But a pox o' those banks that choke up the springs.
> Some mischief is brewing, the project smells rank,
> To shut out the river by raising the bank. (I, 287)

Ironically, with hindsight, we can see that the bank
would have been most beneficial to Ireland.

3

The opportunity for Swift to become involved in
politics on a major scale came with the issue of
Wood's Halfpence in 1722. Ireland had no national
mint and so it was customary for privileged persons
to be handed out patents to coin money. Such a
privileged person was William Wood, an English mine
owner and iron merchant, who received a patent to
coin £100,800 worth of copper coin (this represented
360 tons of copper over fourteen years). It was
claimed that he obtained the patent by paying
£10,000 to the Duchess of Kendal, one of George I's
mistresses. Since Ireland's total currency was about
£400,000, Wood's projected issue amounted to about
a quarter and was generally reckoned to be far in
excess of what the country's economy could stand.
Even Hugh Boulter, the pro-English Primate of
All Ireland, agreed that only £10,000 to £20,000
in copper money was needed. The most persistent
objection raised against the patent was its very
excess. The right of the King to grant such patents
could not be challenged, but contempt had been
shown to the Irish Parliament and there can be no

doubt that giving the patent to Wood was a humiliating reminder of Ireland's dependent status. Swift realised that an act of economic resistance would symbolise a wider rebellion and could be carried out with impunity. He made no move until after the Irish Parliament had shown its determination to resist the patent and, indeed, his efforts would have been futile if the Privy Council and Revenue Commissioners had not withstood English pressure.

Wood was so confident that he would meet with no opposition that he began to circulate his coinage even before a copy of the grant had been sent to Dublin. The government in London ignored the warnings received from Dublin and by the summer of 1723 it became obvious that Wood was proceeding with his plans. In September, a month after the arrival of the Duke of Grafton as Lord Lieutenant, the Irish Parliament was convened and the House of Commons ordered an investigation into Wood's patent, sent a sample of coins for analysis, wrote to the King accusing Wood of fraud and asked that his patent be revoked. This was supported by a similar address from the Lords. Walpole stalled and the matter dragged on into 1724. Wood, meanwhile, did not help his case by boasting of what he would do to force his coinage on the Irish. The letters containing these boasts were made public and implicated the Duke of Grafton. Wood even wrote publicly to a newspaper accusing the London Parliament of misrepresenting the terms of the patent.

It is generally agreed that Swift was asked by influential Irish establishment figures to intervene in the controversy. The idea of proposing a boycott of the coinage was not new, since he had already suggested something similar in his *Proposal for the Universal Use of Irish Manufacture* four years earlier. In 1722 Archbishop King had defined the legal

grounds on which the boycott could be based: the
[78] people had a *right* to refuse the halfpence, and Swift
(masquerading as the Drapier) returns time and again
to this inalienable fact that the law could not force
anybody to accept the money. He chose the mask of
a respectable Protestant shopkeeper, 'M.B., Drapier',
because he so often preferred a pseudonym to anonymity. As the Drapier he could pretend to be a true
spokesman for a large section of ordinary Irish men
and women. In addition, this solid citizen could
provide a well-matched antagonist for William Wood,
and he consistently emphasised Wood's socially low
origins and status. It is also appropriate that the
Drapier, by virtue of his trade, could be expected to
know what was really under people's clothes — a
truly Swiftian metaphor. His main purpose was to
return to the attack on his old political enemies, the
Whig Ministry and the men of money: but the real
battle lay between himself and Walpole.

The British government was forced to order an
enquiry in the spring of 1724 and early in March
Swift moved into action by printing *A Letter to the
Shopkeepers, Tradesmen, Farmers and Common
People of Ireland* in the form of a penny pamphlet.
This first Drapier's Letter was addressed mainly to
the middle-class merchants because it was
necessary for him to persuade these influential
people that they were in danger. He had already
discovered in his *Proposal* that it was quite useless
to exhort people from above and consequently this
first letter plays on the fears of the people to whom
it is addressed. It must have been immediately
obvious to the readers that Swift was the author
since the letter contained a reference to the *Proposal*
and a further Swiftian trademark was present in the
mad mathematics, 'They say Squire Conolly has
sixteen thousand pounds a year. Now if he sends for

his rent to town . . . he must have two hundred and fifty horses to bring up his half year's rent' (X, 7). [79]

From the start the Drapier's appeal is distinctly and deliberately Protestant. The words 'Brass Half-Pence' on the title page would have caused concern among Protestant readers, since 'Brass money' to the Irish Protestant traditionally suggested Stuart tyranny, popish persecution and French invasion. The phrase is used over and over again. This letter was written to alarm the middle-class shopkeepers about the dangers of Wood's halfpence and it is couched in Swift's apparently irrefutable logic: the halfpence will depreciate in value, their number will be limitless, they are so poorly minted that counterfeit money will flood the kingdom. The opening paragraph at once established the manner of attack to be kept up throughout the series:

> What I intend now to say to you is, next to your duty to God and the care of your salvation, of the greatest concern to yourselves and your children; your bread and clothing, and every common necessary of life entirely depend upon it. Therefore I do most earnestly exhort you as men, as Christians, as parents and as lovers of your country, to read this paper with the utmost attention or get it read to you by others, which that you may do at the less expense I have ordered the printer to sell it at the lowest rate (X, 3).

In April an assay of Wood's coins was conducted in London by Sir Isaac Newton, Master of the Mint. His report was leaked to Ireland and, as everyone had expected, it reported that the coins were of good quality. It was widely believed that Wood had deliberately rigged the samples to be analysed. He then made four proposals to quieten the Irish, including a reduction in the amount to be issued.

The second Drapier's Letter did not appear until [80] August 1724 and was addressed to 'Mr Harding the Printer'. It was written, the title page informs us, 'upon the occasion of a paragraph in his newspaper of August 1st relating to Mr Wood's Half-Pence' (X, 13). In his first letter the Drapier had explained Ireland's rights and called on the people individually to refuse the halfpence. In this *Letter to Harding* he aims at stiffening the resolve of the legislature and executive as well as reassuring the populace, and he begins to speak as a citizen of Ireland when he calls for a collective boycott: 'When the evil day is come (if it must come) let us mark and observe those who presume to offer these half-pence in payment. Let their names and trades and places of abode be made public, that everyone may be aware of them as betrayers of their country and confederates with Mr Wood' (X, 23). So the Drapier begins to arouse anger and to direct it towards mass protest. Shortly after its appearance a group of Dublin bankers signed a resolution not to accept the halfpence. The English Privy Council ordered the Commissioners of Revenue to accept and issue Wood's coin without hindrance, but this command was ignored by the Irish executive.

At the end of August or in early September there appeared the third letter, *Some Observations upon a Paper, call'd the Report of the Honourable the Privy-Council in England relating to Wood's Halfpence*, which was directed to 'the nobility and gentry of the kingdom of Ireland'. To suit the occasion, the Drapier becomes more learned and this letter is rather more restrained in tone. However, although this letter is often seen as less effective than the others it also is important because the theme of Irish independence is now out in the open, and what had promised to be merely an economic boycott has now become a political demonstration. The letter contains the famous paragraph:

[81]

> Were not the people of Ireland born as free as those
> of England? How have they forfeited their freedom?
> Is not their Parliament as fair a representative of
> the people as that of England? And hath not their
> Privy Council as great, or a greater share in the ad-
> ministration of public affairs? Are they not subjects
> of the same King? Does not the same sun shine over
> them? And have they not the same God for their
> protector? Am I a freeman in England and do I be-
> come a slave in six hours by crossing the Channel?

There followed a flood of resolutions and signatures
opposing Wood, as men of all classes rushed to show
their determination not to accept the half-pence. On
8 September a huge demonstration took place in
Dublin and citizens marched through the streets with
an effigy of Wood.

Walpole was so unwilling to leave the administration of Ireland any longer in the unreliable hands
of the judiciary that he decided to send the new Lord
Lieutenant, Lord Carteret, to Dublin a year earlier
than he was due to asume office. Swift was well
disposed to Carteret and had kept him informed of the
progress of events in Dublin. Carteret had been
Walpole's rival for power, and since the Duchess of
Kendal, Wood's patron, had supported Walpole, it is
not surprising that Carteret should have been
sympathetic to the anti-Walpole cause. Knowing
that even his good relations with Carteret would
not prevent this much abler Lord Lieutenant from
being forced to act against him, Swift moved quickly
to finish his fourth letter, *A Letter to the Whole
People of Ireland*, which was published on 21 October
before Carteret landed. The tone of the letter moves
between the lordly and the impudent as for the first
time the Drapier identifies himself with Molyneux

and addresses the whole nation. The Drapier names
and indicts those in high office who had obtained
their positions corruptly. When he writes 'all government without the consent of the governed is the very
definition of slavery' (X, 63), he is as near as he could
safely get to open and deliberate defiance of the
English claim to legislate for a dependent Ireland.

As soon as Carteret had read the letter he sum-
moned a meeting of the Privy Council and made it
clear that he regarded it as treasonable. All members
'owned their abhorrence of the pamphlet, as seditious
and of dangerous consequences' (despite the private
views of many of them) and a majority of the Council
wanted to have Harding arrested and to issue a
proclamation offering a reward of £300 to anyone
who should discover the Drapier's identity. A number
of passages were marked by Carteret as being particularly offensive when he reported to Walpole on
28 October 1724. When an order for the prosecution
of Harding the printer was drawn up, several members
refused to sign it, and even those who signed the proclamation offering a reward for the discovery of the
Drapier's identity cunningly sought to avoid involvement by revising it to show that they were not against
the letter as a whole but against only *parts* of it. No
one was inclined to attack the author and his praises
were sung in the streets to a suitable quotation from
the Old Testament, 'And the people said unto Saul,
shall Jonathan die, who hath wrought this great
salvation in Israel? God forbid: as the Lord liveth
there shall not one hair of his head fall to the ground;
for he hath wrought with God this day: So the people
rescued Jonathan and he died not.' Archbishop King
then called on Carteret to tell him that the Drapier
was about to unmask himself, but Swift had in fact
gone even further in his ideas in his fifth letter, *A
Letter to the Lord Chancellor Midleton*, which was

nearly finished. Carteret warned King that any further letters would be a serious matter and Swift withdrew publication. On 7 November Harding was arrested and while he was awaiting trial Swift circulated on 14 November an anonymous paper, *Seasonal Advice to the Grand-Jury, concerning the Bill preparing against the Printer of the preceding Letter*, addressed to those who were to examine Harding and noting 'several things maturely to be considered by those gentlemen' (X, 69). The Grand Jury met on 21 November under Lord Chief Justice Whitshed and two other judges. The jury refused to convict and so Whitshed dismissed them and brought in a new jury, but before Harding could be brought before them the Michaelmas Term ended and he was released. On the last day of the term this second jury also refused to condemn *Seasonal Advice*, and instead singled out 'all such persons as have attempted, or shall endeavour by fraud, or otherwise, to impose the said halfpence upon us' (X, 75). It is thought that this was itself instigated by Swift.

The enemy were now in full retreat but Swift pursued them relentlessly in verse. He reserved the full force for Lord Chief Justice Whitshed. In the poem 'Whitshed's motto on his coach' Swift plays ironically with the motto 'Libertas et natale solum' ('Liberty and my native country') as he begins to address Whitshed:

Libertas et natale solum;
Fine words; I wonder where you stole 'um. (I, 348)

He continues with great vigour:

Libertas bears a large import;
First; how to swagger in a court;
And, secondly, to show my fury
Against an uncomplying jury. (I, 348)

In the same year Swift wrote 'Verses on the upright
judge, who condemned the Drapier's printer'. He also
attacked Wood in 'A serious poem upon William
Wood, brazier, tinker, hardwareman, coiner, counter-
feiter, founder and esquire':

> When foes are o'ercome, we preserve them from
> slaughter,
> To be hewers of wood and drawers of water,
> Now, although to draw water is not very good,
> Yet we all should rejoice to be hewers of Wood.

(I, 334)

In these comparatively light poems can be seen the
familiar note of Swift's poetry: the ironic humour in
the titles and the liberal use of puns in his treatment
of Wood, whose very name was, of course, heaven-
sent.

On 31 December Harding printed the fifth letter,
*To the Right Honourable the Lord Viscount
Molesworth*, which became Swift's celebration of
his triumph over the judiciary. It seems that he
intended the letter to be his last and after it was
published the Irish sat back to wait for England's
verdict. This was eventually announced by the Irish
Privy Council on 26 August 1725 and it was to the
effect that Wood had surrendered the patent. 'The
work is done,' wrote Swift, 'and there is no more
need of the Drapier' (iii, 93). Even after his patent
was withdrawn, the attack on Wood and London
continued as a small group in Dublin cleverly inserted
in the address of thanks to the King the words 'in
his great wisdom', referring to the King's withdrawal
of the patent. This phrase was then debated for two
days when its implications were understood.

The Drapier's Letters had been a triumph for
Swift. He had scored a notable success in political
terms and become 'the Hibernian Patriot', thus

ensuring his place in Irish history. In literary terms the *Letters* gave him the opportunity to perfect the [85] mask form (of the Drapier) which he was at the same time using as Gulliver. He had also acquired a sure sense of audience with the *Letters*. He knew *who* he was writing for in each letter and tailored contents and tone to that audience. This enabled him to become a popular writer on a larger scale than he had achieved with his previous work. So *The Drapier's Letters* provided him with a very successful practice ground for the Irish public writing and preaching which he continued for the rest of his life.

The *Letters* had the psychological effect of promoting some kind of unity between the Anglo-Irish and the Irish people. The hostile Archbishop Boulter wrote 'that the people of every religion, country and party here, are alike set against Wood's halfpence, and that their agreement in this has had a very unhappy influence on the state of this nation, by bringing on intimacies between Papists and Jacobites and the Whigs, who before had no correspondence with them' (5, 95). Swift and the Irish, however, had only a temporary victory in the war with London. The main political result of the battle was to force Walpole to take steps to ensure that such a confrontation could never happen again. There was no great benefit for Ireland since the constitutional position remained unchanged until 1782, and restraints on Irish trade continued. In addition, Walpole sent a new Primate to ensure that all significant church vacancies were filled by supporters of the English interest. Wood was given a pension of £24,000 as compensation and, with an irony to match that of the Drapier, Walpole drew the money from the funds of the Irish establishment. Swift continued to take an interest in Irish affairs although he still tended to reject the label of patriot as when, for example, he wrote to Pope in 1728, 'What I do is [86] owing to perfect rage and resentment, and the mortifying sight of slavery, folly and baseness about me, among which I am forced to live' (iii, 289). By the time he wrote his *Short View of the State of Ireland* in 1728 he could feel only resignation, 'One thing I know, that when the hen is starved to death there will be no more golden eggs' (XII, 12).

4

The World-Besotted Traveller

Less than a month after writing that the Drapier was no longer needed Swift was writing a long (and now famous) letter to Pope: 'I have employed my time (besides ditching) in finishing correcting, amending and transcribing my travels in four parts complete, newly augmented, and intended for the press when the world shall deserve them, or rather, when a printer shall be found brave enough to venture his ears' (iii, 102). He then proceeds to his much-quoted intention that 'the chief end I propose to myself in all my labours is to vex the world rather than divert it'. He follows this with his famous statement about the rationality of man which was to be at the core of *Gulliver's Travels*:

> . . . when you think of the world give it one lash the more at my request. I have ever hated all nations, professions and communities, and all my love is towards individuals. For instance, I hate the tribe of lawyers, but I love Counsellor such a one, Judge such a one; for so with physicians (I will not speak of my own trade), soldiers, English, Scots, French and the rest. But principally I hate and detest that animal called man, although I heartily love John, Peter, Thomas and so forth. This is the system upon which I have governed myself many years . . . and so I shall go on till I have done with them. I have got materials towards

a treatise proving the falsity of that definition *animal rationale* and to show it should be only *rationis capax*. Upon this great foundation of misanthropy (though not Timon's manner) the whole building of my travels is erected. And I never will have peace of mind till all honest men are of my opinion . . .' (iii, 103).

Thus Swift is attacking the view of man not as a rational animal (*'animal rationale'*) but as an animal *capable* of reason (*'rationis capax'*); for Swift a considerable difference between theory and fact.

He did little else for the next few months except prepare *Gulliver's Travels* for the printer. On 26 November 1725 he wrote again to Pope, looking forward to meeting him again, and returning to the purpose of *Gulliver's Travels:* 'I tell you after all that I do not hate mankind. It is *vous autres* who hate them because you would have them reasonable animals and are angry for being disappointed' (iii, 118).

He travelled to England with the manuscript in early March 1726, spent some time with Pope and was presented to the Prince of Wales, who maintained a rival court virtually in opposition to that of his father. In April 1726 Swift met Walpole and put forward his views on Irish liberty: 'my principal design was to set him right, not only for the service of Ireland, but likewise of England, and of his own administration: (iii, 132). He had two interviews with Walpole, the first at Walpole's invitation, the second 'at my desire for an hour, wherein we differed in every point' (iii, 144).

He thoroughly enjoyed the visit to England, meeting old friends, but a cloud hung over everything with the news from Dublin that Stella was extremely ill:

What you tell me of Mrs Johnson I have long expected with great oppression and heaviness of heart. We have been perfect friends these thirty-five years. Upon my advice they both came to Ireland and have been ever since my constant companions. And the remainder of my life will be a very melancholy scene when one of them is gone whom I most esteemed upon the score of every good quality that can possibly recommend a human creature. I have these two months seen through Miss Dingley's disguises, and indeed, ever since I left you my heart is so sunk that I have not been the same man, nor ever shall be again, but drag on a wretched life till it shall please God to call me away (iii, 141).

He left for Ireland in August, before the publication of *Gulliver's Travels*.

2

The idea of the book began with the Scriblerus Club. The club's members intended to write jointly the memoirs of their creation Martin Scriblerus, but little progress was made and the other members left to Swift the initiative in writing them. Voyages were popular reading at the time and perhaps the most popular were those of William Dampier, whose plain, factual reporting was obviously a model which Swift followed in *Gulliver's Travels* and there are many parallels between Dampier's travels and those of Lemuel Gulliver. Dampier had travelled to the East Indies and the north coast of Australia and his *Voyage round the World* appeared in 1697. Swift must also have known Woodes Rogers's *A Cruising Voyage round the World* (1712). *Robinson Crusoe* had already been a great success in 1719 and Swift, having considered the matter for a long time, followed suit. It has been said that he wrote *Gulliver's*

Travels in order to turn *Robinson Crusoe* upside
down although he pretended not to know Defoe,
'one of these authors (the fellow that was pilloried,
I have forgot his name)' (II, 113). In April 1721
he wrote 'I am now writing a history of my travels,
which will be a large volume, and gives account of
countries hitherto unknown; but they go on slowly
for want of health and humour' (ii, 381). The first
two book were written in 1721–2 and the fourth
book in 1723. Fortunately, during 1722–4 he was
reasonably free of his giddiness and deafness. In
January 1724 he wrote 'I have left the country of
horses, and am in the flying island, where I shall not
stay long, and my two last journeys will be soon
over' (iii, 5). The third book was not completed until
1725. In August 1725 he wrote from Quilca to his
friend Ford 'I have finished my travels, and I am now
transcribing them. They are admirable things, and will
wonderfully mend the world' (iii, 87).

The circumstances surrounding the actual publication of the book are typical of Swift's subterfuge.
The London printer Benjamin Motte received a letter
dated 8 August 1726 from one Richard Sympson,
who offered for sale a copy of the travels of his
cousin Mr Lemuel Gulliver. Sympson assured Motte
'I have shown them to several persons of great
judgment and distinction, who are confident that
they will sell very well; and although some parts of
this and the following volumes may be thought in one
or two places to be a little satirical, yet it is agreed
they will give no offence . . .' (iii, 153). After an
exchange of letters between Motte and Sympson the
manuscript was left on the publisher's doorstep and
Motte published the first edition on 28 October 1726.
Two editions followed in 1726 and two more in
1727. Eventually, Swift, dissatisfied with the text,
corrected the version later published in 1735 as part

of his complete *Works*. The author of the *Travels* was identified on the title page as Lemuel Gulliver, 'first a [91] surgeon, then a captain of several ships'. A few readers knew the true author's identity but despite the immediate success of the book Swift kept up the pretence that he hadn't written it. Ten days after it was published Gay reported to him, ''Tis generally said that you are the author, but I am told the book-seller declares he knows not from what hand it came. From the highest to the lowest it is universally read, from the cabinet council to the nursery' (iii, 182).

Gulliver's Travels has remained popular at all times since its publication although it is customary to note that it has also survived in abridged form as a chil-dren's classic, usually without Book Four and with other obvious cuts. Michael Foot calls it 'a perpetual unfinished argument' (*38*, 200) and notes how it was treasured as a seditious tract by the early nineteenth-century radicals Hazlitt, Cobbett, Leigh Hunt and Godwin, who, he suggests, felt its relevance for them in the midst of a major war. Many claims have been advanced for the book and it is not without its relevance today. Michael Foot, a great admirer of Swift, has described it as 'still the most powerful of pacifist pamphlets' (*38*, 228) and suggested at the 1981 Labour Party Conference that it should be required reading for the Tory government of Margaret Thatcher.

There have been many fierce discussions about the 'meaning' of the work and in particular about the fourth book: such arguments are inevitable because of Swift's ironic style. There is a long-standing debate about where the author stands in relation to the ideas of Book Four and to a lesser extent about the political references in the whole work. One of the difficulties with Swift is that his technique is to clear the ground and not necessarily to go on to plant any seed, so

the reader is often unclear about his actual standpoint.
[92] This is the problem of perspective which is central to
Gulliver's Travels and to much of his work. The book
is not a novel in the usual sense of the term and so
there can be no expectation of plot, character
development and other familiar features of the post-
eighteenth-century novel. Some critics have asked
whether the book can even be great satire if there
is so much fundamental disagreement about it. It has
to be treated as a moral fable and the reader must
exercise great care in his approach.

This, however, is not to deny the great enjoyment
which we get from it and it is this enjoyment which
is the mark of any book that survives as a children's
classic.

3

The story is well known. In a series of sea journeys
Lemuel Gulliver finds himself alone in strange countries: he is shipwrecked and lands in Lilliput, he is
accidentally left on the shore of Brobdingnag, he is
captured by pirates and lands in Laputa, and a
mutinous crew cast him ashore in Houyhnhnmland.
Swift cleverly makes use of a few pages of apparently
authentic travel description at the start of each book
to make plausible the adventures of Gulliver. Although
Gulliver is really a different *persona* in each book,
Swift patiently yet skilfully in a few pages sketches in
his background, the circumstances of his voyage and
the events leading up to his arrival in strange countries. The presence of vaguely defined maps (at a
time when maps were usually imprecise and sometimes fictional) again gives apparent authenticity. In
Lilliput the gentle giant Gulliver is among people
one-twelfth his size; in Brobdingnag the sycophantic
midget Gulliver seeks to ingratiate himself with

people twelve times his size. In Laputa, Balnibarbi, Glubbdubdrib and Luggnag, Gulliver is the same size as the inhabitants but merely a spectator of their odd goings on. In the powerful final book Gulliver is torn between the bestial Yahoos, whom he resembles in appearance, and the cold-blooded rational Houyhnhnms, whom he aspires to join. To a greater or lesser extent in all the books Gulliver discusses the state of England and the country he is in, drawing comparisons and making comments on both, so that the work resembles the traditional Utopian fable where writers go outside their own country to examine a potential future: Thomas More's *Utopia* (1551), Samuel Butler's *Erewhon* (1872), H.G. Wells's *A Modern Utopia* (1905) or Aldous Huxley's *Brave New World* (1932). Swift includes many references to the contemporary English and European scene: he comments on Walpole and his government, he derides members of parliament, party factions, religious bickering, peers, lawyers and doctors. He attacks standing armies, the spread of sophisticated weapons of destruction, colonialism. There is a danger of turning the book into a patchwork quilt of disjointed ideas and social comment.

The first two books emphasise physical differences. Swift has great fun with the giant Gulliver's relations with the tiny Lilliputians. His ingenuity is exercised over how much food Gulliver will consume each day, how Gulliver will communicate with his hosts and even how Gulliver will exercise his bodily functions. In Brobdingnag the tiny Gulliver gets into all kinds of scrapes and is attacked by giant wasps, a giant dwarf, a dog, a monkey, a frog and by birds. He is sexually humiliated by the court maids of honour in their dressing-room and he sees close up the hideousness of their skins (as he sees elsewhere the huge sores of beggars).

The third book is a mixture of strange experiences but it is chiefly remembered for the crazy projectors of the Grand Academy of Lagado, who resemble the stereotype of the mad scientist. They are trying to extract sunshine out of cucumbers, to restore human excrement to its original food and to make ice into gunpowder. A 'most ingenious architect' had found a way to build houses by starting at the roof and working downwards, which he justified because copied from bees and spiders. Another projector was saving money by using pigs to plough the ground, but first he had to bury 'at six inches distance and eight deep, a quantity of acorns, dates, chestnuts and other mast or vegetables whereof these animals are fondest' (XI, 180). A mad physician is curing diseases by the use of a bellows to pump out the illness from patients. Swift might at first appear to be out of step with progress in his rejection of the new scientists, but, as Patrick Reilly reminds us, Bertrand Russell praised Book Three for showing how science can go wrong.[1] In Book Three Swift's frenzied energy is given great play. But there is also a serious side since the flying island of Laputa hovers over the subject island of Balnibarbi, crushing any opposition by either dropping on it or hovering over it so that sun and rain are cut off. Here Swift may well have been thinking of the relationship between Ireland and England. Balnibarbi is a colony of Laputa and the inhabitants suffer from the relationship, 'The people in the streets walked fast, looked wild, their eyes fixed, and were generally in rags . . . neither did I observe any expectation either of corn or grass, although the soil appeared to be excellent' (XI, 174). Lord Munodi, the Governor of the capital of Lagado, has been identified as Viscount Midleton, the Lord Chancellor of Ireland, who, although a Whig, opposed the imposition of Wood's Halfpence; but the character has also been identified with Oxford and Bolingbroke.

Perhaps the most vivid inhabitants of the lands in [95] the third book are the Struldbruggs of Luggnag, who can never die. Gulliver, our naive and idealistic representative, cries out 'Happy nation where every child hath at least a chance for being immortal! Happy people who enjoy so many living examples of ancient virtue, and have masters ready to instruct them in the wisdom of all former ages! But happiest beyond all comparison are those excellent Struldbruggs, who being born exempt from that universal calamity of human nature, have their minds free and disengaged, without the weight and depression of spirits caused by the continual apprehension of death' (XI, 208). But the real state of the Struldbruggs is very different. At eighty 'they are looked on as dead in law' (XI, 212); 'At ninety they lose their teeth and hair' (XI, 213); because the language, like English, is always changing, 'the Struldbruggs of one age do not understand those of another' (XI, 213). Gulliver eventually decided, 'they were the most mortifying sight I ever beheld, and the women more horrible than the men' (XI, 214). He has learnt his lesson.

Book Four consists of the steady progression of Gulliver towards the Houyhnhnms while he discusses England and the Houyhnhnm state. The Houyhnhnms are ruled entirely by reason and the Yahoos live by their lower nature. As Swift said, 'the lower powers are gotten uppermost'. Gulliver is trapped between them, but by the time he returns to England (as he does after each voyage) he thinks he is a Houyhnhnm and cannot bear the presence of human beings.

The way we see the person of Gulliver (or see *through* him) has an important bearing on our reading of his travels. Swift makes no attempt at a consistent character; in Lilliput he loses royal support by stick-

ing to his ideas (he is a person we admire); in
Brobdingnag he is an unpleasant toady currying
royal favour. In Lilliput he resolves never to trust
princes or ministers again after he has been betrayed
by them; but in subsequent voyages he is once again
in deep discussion with them. In each book Gulliver
is supposed to start again and remember nothing
from his previous voyages, but internal references
to earlier voyages prove this untrue. There is a good
deal of confusion at the end of each voyage which
is made worse because at the end of Book Four
Gulliver is apparently insane (either temporarily or
permanently) yet he is able to set down his earlier
adventures. But obviously we cannot explain his
behaviour among his family at the end of Book
Four in psychological terms because it is simply a
satirical device. To repeat, this is not the way of the
conventional novel: it is fruitless to ask whether
Gulliver at the end of his voyages is a man with his
eyes opened or a man driven insane by his adventures. He is not to be treated as a man, but more as
something to reflect ideas and comments, to refract
the experiences offered to him.

The most helpful way of looking at Gulliver is to
see him as a victim of alienation. It is relevant to cite
again Swift's own Anglo-Irish dilemma of identification and to see a certain parallel between Swift
and Gulliver. But Gulliver is clearly brainwashed.
Denis Donoghue spelt out this most interesting and
most contemporary view of Gulliver in a radio talk
on the 250th anniversary of the book (23, 578-9).
Since the Second World War most people know
something of brainwashing, 'the systematic and
often forcible elimination from a person's mind
of all established ideas, especially political ideas, so
that another set may take their place'. It can be
effected by physical torture, or, as we have seen in

recent years, by more subtle psychological methods such as sensory deprivation, which brings about a lack of orientation on the part of the victim. If a subject resists, then the coercion will need to be stronger. Gulliver's resistance is very slight since he is already ripe for brainwashing when he sets out on his travels. We know at the start that he has some competence in navigation and elementary medicine, but beyond this he seems incapable of dealing with the monsters he meets. He is very much the empiricist, who can only deal with experiences that can be measured or computed. He has no interest in what lies beneath the surface since it cannot be seen. He is xenophobic, chauvinistic, sometimes arrogant and almost always lacking in feeling. The humour in the book comes often from our watching Gulliver's mind, programmed to deal only with humdrum events, struggling to mediate to the reader the most amazing and bizarre occurrences. We cannot trust him to help us to understand the experiences he goes through. The brainwashing of Gulliver is accomplished by subtle means. He is physically disorientated in the first two books, where he has to adjust to being twelve times bigger then twelve time smaller than his hosts. In Book Three he is confused by the whirling scenes of madness around him, and then in Book Four he is morally disorientated, so that by the end he has lost his original identity and actually believes himself to be a horse.

One of the most effective scenes in this process is at the end of Book Two. It is not an incident which can be easily described since the reader must go through it with Gulliver and suspend belief. Gulliver is in his specially made box which is virtually a room-sized cage, usually carried by a Brobdingnagian lifting the box by putting his finger through the ring on top. A bird flies off with the box and drops it in the ocean. Gulliver hears a ship nearby, 'a trampling over

my head, and somebody calling through the hole
with a loud voice in the English tongue: If there
be anybody below let them speak' (XI, 143). It is
very hard to make the mental transition here and
the reader wonders whether he has become small
with Gulliver or, identifying with the Brobdingnagians,
has viewed Gulliver throughout the book as a midget.
We are as much off balance as Gulliver and the ship's
crew. It is very similar to the end of Golding's *Lord
of the Flies*, when we follow the boy Ralph along
the sea shore and he falls at the feet of an apparently
enormous naval officer. Suddenly we resume our
adult heights and Ralph shrinks back to being a
small schoolboy. By the end of Book Four Gulliver
has become totally enchanted by Houyhnhnmland.
People can be more readily enchanted by what they
themselves imagine, and Gulliver is no exception.
He sets up the apparatus for his own brainwashing.
By the end of Book Four, like Winston at the end
of *Nineteen Eighty Four*, he could say 'he loved
Big Brother'. 'Far more shockingly than *Nineteen
Eighty Four*, Swift implies that the few cubic centi-
metres within the skull which we so confidently
proclaim the realm of freedom, an inviolable zone,
a no-go area to violence and intimidation, are as
casually penetrated as our vulnerable bodies, minds
bent as easily as limbs are broken,' writes Patrick
Reilly (*42*, 17).

Gullivers Travels then, is about perspective in its
fullest sense. Gulliver, who has no personality, is a
chameleon, who depends on the circumstances in
which he is placed. Swift appears greatly interested
in problems of perspective, in standpoints. It has been
suggested that one of the reasons for his interest in
perspective was the powerful effect upon him and his
contemporaries of Newton's discoveries in the field
of optics. The microscope and the telescope exercised

considerable interest at the time, and the first two books of *Gulliver's Travels* are clearly a view of man seen from either end of the telescope. One of Swift's favourite tricks was to present abstract ideas in some concrete form and an excellent example of this is found soon after Gulliver's arrival in Lilliput. Generations of children have enjoyed the description of the contents of Gulliver's pockets as seen through Lilliputian eyes. This is a further example of perspective. Familiar objects seen in an unusual light, from an unfamiliar angle, become difficult to identify; the same goes for ideas. So the 'great piece of coarse cloth', the 'prodigious bundle of white thin substances', the 'hollow pillar of iron . . . fastened to a strange piece of timber', the 'two black pillars', the 'globe, half silver', become a handkerchief, letters, pistol, shaving implements, pocket watch (XI, 34-5). This simple device of Swift's illustrates his preoccupation (also seen in the scatological poems) with making us take a fresh look at familiar objects and ideas. This technique has been recently renewed in Craig Raine's poem 'A Martian sends a postcard home'.

4.

Gulliver's Travels is also a political tract and an understanding of the underlying issues of the time does provide an added dimension. For instance, Swift passes comment on the orders of chivalry. The blue, red and green ribbons, which are prizes for those who leap over the Emperor of Lilliput's stick or creep under it, obviously represent the Orders of the Garter, the Bath and the Thistle. The heir to the throne of Lilliput is inclined to the High Heels, whereas his father favours the Low Heels (the size of one's heels indicating the party one adhered to). Lilliput (England) is at war with its neighbour Blefuscu

(France). Gulliver's impeachment by the government [100] of Lilliput echoes that of Oxford and Bolingbroke by the Whigs after 1714. Since Swift had also defended the four *Whig* ministers impeached in 1701 by the Tories we can deduce that by the time he wrote this book he felt that the party spirit in politics led often to persecution and injustice. The dreadful consequences following the battle over breaking eggs at the big end or the little end remind the reader of the Reformation and the disputes over transubstantiation and the primacy of the Pope. Though there are many such political parallels, first comprehensively identified by Sir Charles Firth in 1919,[2] there are also many discrepancies. Swift more generally than particularly shows his distaste for factions and party men and he does not so much show his opposition to Walpole specifically as his feelings about politicians in general. He had had, after all, years of exposure to politicians of all shades both in London and in Dublin and his final scathing dismissal of them came later in 'The Legion Club'.

In all the books Gulliver explores the state of England directly and indirectly. Reldresal, the Principal Secretary (quite possibly Swift's friend Lord Carteret) tells Gulliver about the condition of the state of Lilliput. In his description we see thinly disguised the condition of England; the educational system is ruthlessly designed to perpetuate existing class divisions and despite its efforts Lilliput has a violent faction at home and dangers of invasion from abroad. There are clever inversions used in the description of Lilliput by which the state of England is commented on: 'In choosing persons of all employments, they have more regard to good morals than to great abilities' (XI, 59), 'the disbelief of a Divine Providence renders a man uncapable of holding any public station.' But Lilliput is, in general, a country not to be admired. The educational system is clinical, the children are brought up away from home and the class system is assiduously reinforced. The country is peopled by a race of unpleasant pygmies, who eventually impeach the benevolent Gulliver in much the same terms as Swift's friends had been impeached by the Whigs. Gulliver escapes sentence of death which, after cold-blooded debate, is commuted to blinding and he finally avoids execution of sentence by fleeing the country. Once again, the universality of *Gulliver's Travels* can be seen as modern readers are reminded of the treatment of political prisoners and fallen leaders in many countries today.

In Book Two Gulliver describes Brobdingnag and is then questioned about England. To atone for his size he offers a panegyric in praise of England but the King sees through this and his questioning exposes the real situation. Something of the flavour of this panegyric can be seen in, for example, Gulliver's description of the House of Lords, which consisted of 'persons of the noblest blood . . . I described that extraordinary care always taken of their education in arts and arms, to qualify them for being counsellors born to the king and kingdom . . . That these were the ornament and bulwark of the kingdom' (XI, 128). The Commons 'were all principal gentlemen, *freely* picked and culled out by the people themselves, for their great abilities, and love of their country, to represent the wisdom of the whole nation' (XI, 128). The King soon deflates Gulliver's naive panegyric with apparently innocent questions such as 'whether, a stranger with a strong purse might not influence the vulgar voters to choose him before their own landlord' and 'what qualifications were necessary in those who are to be created new Lords; whether the humour of the Prince, a sum of money to a Court Lady, or a Prime Minister, or a design of strengthening a party

opposite to the public interest, ever happened to
[102] be motives in those advancements' (XI, 129). Swift's
technique is clever. The King cannot understand why
Gulliver and the English should group people according to religion and politics, 'He said, he knew no
reason, why those who entertain opinion prejudicial
to the public should be obliged to change, or should
not be obliged to conceal them' (XI, 131). This, of
course, was Swift's own position. In *Thoughts on
Religion* he wrote 'Every man, as a member of the
Commonwealth, ought to be content with the possession of his own opinion in private, without
perplexing his neighbours or disturbing the public'
(XI, 261). Poor Gulliver totally fails to convince
the King of the worth of England, 'My little friend
Grildrig; you have made a most admirable panegyric
upon your country. You have clearly proved that
ignorance, idleness, and vice are the proper ingredients
for qualifying a legislator' (XI, 132). Gulliver describes
a Brobdingnag which seems to have many attractive
features, but he himself is so deluded that he is
incapable of seeing them, 'The learning of this people
is very defective, consisting only in morality, history,
poetry and mathematics, wherein they must be
allowed to excel' (XI, 136). The more Gulliver comments on Brobdingnag the more we realise that we
are on the side of the inhabitants. All their 'faults' are
really virtues and Gulliver is simply being as short-
sighted as his stature necessitates.

In Houyhnhnmland Gulliver is again questioned
about England, but this time he is quite explicit in
his references to specific people and events. In addition
to his comments on war he also delivers attacks on
the legal profession, medicine and prime ministers.
There is a humorous account of the way lawyers
work, 'a society of men . . . bred up from their youth
in the art of proving . . . that white is black, and black

is white according as they are paid' (XI, 248). As well as lawyers, there was 'another sort of people, who got [103] their livelihood by attending the sick. . . .' (XI, 253). Swift almost parodies his own earlier treatment of the Aeolists in his description of the way doctors treat all diseases as rising from repletion, thus necessitating purges and evacuation. He reserves a special spleen for his attack on chief ministers, a species which 'is usually governed by a decayed wench or favourite footman, who are the tunnels through which all graces are conveyed' (XI, 256).

There is an important discussion in Book Two between Gulliver and the King on the discovery of gunpowder. In a last vain attempt to ingratiate himself with the King, who has already given his opinion of Gulliver's kind as 'the most pernicious race of little odious vermin that nature ever suffered to crawl upon the surface of the earth' (XI, 132). Gulliver gives a graphic description of the discovery of gunpowder and a horrifying description of the effects of its use and results. All this is presented in a tone of panegyric and with some relish and Gulliver offers to disclose the secrets to the King's advantage. He is so self-deceived that he simply cannot understand why 'The King was struck with horror at the description' (XI, 134). The King told him 'he would rather lose half his kingdom than be privy to such a secret, which he commanded me, as I valued my life, never to mention any more' (XI, 135). The modern reader thinks here of the moral dilemma which confronted the scientists who discovered nuclear fission and who had then to decide whether to reveal their discoveries to politicians and to consider what their own involvement would be in any resulting deaths. Brecht has presented this dilemma in an oblique but powerful way in his play *The Life of Galilei* (1947), and on a less dramatic level the debate is presented fictionally in C.P. Snow's *The New Men* (1954); and the [104] recent television series *Oppenheimer* showed the involvement of a single scientist. In a vein which would command much support today, the King continues that 'whoever could make two ears of corn, or two blades of grass to grow upon a spot of ground where only one grew before, would deserve better of mankind, and do more essential service to his country, than the whole race of politicians put together' (XI, 135-6).

In Book Two Swift had taken the standard Tory view in opposition to standing armies, a view he had expressed earlier in the *Examiner*: 'A general and his army are servants hired by the civil power to act as they are directed from thence' (III, 43). By Book Four he has moved on to a general indictment of war in absolute terms and Gulliver clearly states Swift's own views. The causes of war are the ambition of princes, the corruption of ministers, differences of opinion. Gulliver explains that 'a soldier is a Yahoo hired to kill in cold blood as many of his own species, who have never offended him, as possibly he can' (XI, 246-7). There is a matter-of-fact description of the 'art' of war delivered by a Gulliver who might possibly be the victim of Swift's irony as he had been in Book Two, since the description he gives is so full of relish ('the dead bodies drop down in pieces from the clouds, to the great diversion of all the spectators') (XI, 247). The Houyhnhnm master is appalled at this description and shows the same revulsion which the King of Brobdingnag had shown to Gulliver: 'He said, whoever understood the nature of Yahoos might easily believe it possible for so vile an animal to be capable of every action I had named . . .' (X, 247).

In addition to writing about party politics in England Swift also wrote about Ireland. Gulliver offers a description of how unknown lands are annexed and 'a new dominion acquired with a title by *divine right*' (XI, 294). Then various atrocities [105] and illegal acts follow and this 'is a *modern colony* sent to convert and civilise an idolatrous and barbarous people' (XI, 294). Swift then devotes a heavily ironic paragraph to disclaiming that this description 'doth by no means affect the British nation, who may be an example to the whole world for their wisdom, care, and justice in planting colonies . . .' (XI, 294).

The major concern of *Gulliver's Travels*, which is pride, places the work in line with most of Swift's work. In Book One, for example, we read of pride in the achievements of human society especially through the eyes of Gulliver. In Book Two he is ridiculed and his own pride in his country and even in his own personal morality is removed; but he manages to retain his intellectual position. In Book Three Swift attacks the intellectual achievements of man, and the Royal Society in particular; all the discoveries and research have led nowhere. In Book Four it is reason, the last support of pride, which is examined. Central to the whole of Gulliver's experiences is a long paragraph devoted to his diatribe against pride. The Houyhnhnms have no name for this 'vice' and Gulliver protests that he has no patience for 'a lump of deformity and diseases both in body and mind, smitten with pride . . .' (XI, 296).

A good deal of the discussion about Book Four of *Gulliver's Travels* centres on the fact that the Houyhnhnms are ruled completely by reason whereas the Yahoos have none. Is Book Four a plea for reason or is it the exposure of the absurd consequences of too much reason? Do the horses represent Swift's ideals, or attitudes which he wants to satirise? Certainly Swift was unhappy with a prevailing view that 'Reason alone is sufficient to govern a rational creature' and he attacked this in his sermons. In his

sermon *On the Trinity* he wrote, 'Reason itself is true
[106] and just, but the reason of every particular man is
weak and wavering, perpetually swayed and turned
by his interests, his passions and his vices' (IX, 166).
As recently as forty years ago most critics believed
that Swift supported Gulliver in his apparent
obsession with reason but today the matter is viewed
differently. One must certainly ask whether the
Houyhnhnms are to be seen as an ideal race or
whether they represent the ridiculing by Swift of
the eighteenth-century rationalists. One thing
which is certain is that Swift is attacking man's
arrogant assumption in pretending to reason as he
had made clear in his famous letter to Pope just
before he crossed to England with the manuscript
of *Gulliver's Travels.* So man wavers between Yahoos
and Houyhnhnms and he contains each aspect within
himself. When a lascivious female Yahoo (red-haired
perhaps to remind us of Swift's bitter enemy the
Duchess of Somerset) is physically attracted to
Gulliver he is appalled that she should think him
one of her own kind. Swift no doubt remembered
stories of African women and male apes in travellers'
tales from Africa — stories which he would have
rejected as contrary to nature. Gulliver's alienation
from the Houyhnhnms in Book Four has been seen
as a reminder of Swift's own position of alienation
as an Anglo-Irishman out of place in both Dublin
and London. Gulliver cannot integrate himself into
their society even though he is able to pass for a
Houyhnhnm in many ways.

Another way of looking at Book Four is to see it
in terms of the working out of a conflict between
the followers of the philosophies of Hobbes and
Locke. The Yahoo would be Hobbesian man, whose
life is 'nasty, brutish and short', governed by passions
and always seeking his own advantage and pursuing

pleasure and avoiding pain. The Houyhnhnms are Lockeian men, living together, according to reason, [107] without a common superior and with mutual benevolence. But they more surely represent Shaftesbury's notions of innate virtue, natural religion, harmony and reason. The doctrine of original sin was under attack at the time and it has been argued that the Yahoos are an example of the results of Original Sin and man's fall from Grace.

Perhaps the most interesting approach to Book Four is to see it in terms of Swift's ambivalent attitude towards Ireland. Put bluntly, one has to ask whether the Yahoos represent the native Irish. Swift, naturally, would not be *attacking* the latter, but presenting them ironically in the way that the English government or Irish absentee landlords or place-seeking politicians living in Ireland might have viewed them. Swift himself described the appalling state of the Irish, 'the poorer sort of our natives . . . live in the utmost ignorance, barbarity and poverty, giving themselves wholly up to idleness, nastiness and thievery' and he asked whether anything could be done 'to reduce this uncultured people from that idle, savage, beastly, thievish manner of life.'³ But he goes on to state the cause of this state of affairs as 'the poverty and slavery they suffer from their inhuman neighbours, and the base corrupt spirits of too many of the chief gentry' (iv, 51). It is not difficult then, to see the Houyhnhnms as the oppressors in Ireland. The associations with horses were many: not least, of course, that a Catholic was forbidden under the Penal Laws to own a horse worth more than £5. Horses were loved by many of the aristocracy at the time, portrait painting of horses flourished and many of Swift's aristocratic contemporaries were more concerned to have their horses painted than their families and, no doubt, most horses were better housed in Ireland than the native Irish.

Then there is the celebrated remark of the Irish-born [108] Duke of Wellington who, when asked if he were Irish, replied, 'If I were born in a stable, would that make me a horse?' Is it perhaps too fanciful to speculate, since we have no tape-recordings to help us, whether the curious neighing voices of the horses were intended to resemble the speech of the English and Anglo-Irish oppressors, or at least a parody of that speech? Swift hated the brogue and retained the old-fashioned pronunciations current in Ireland.[4] He advised gentlemen not to visit England upon pain of being ridiculous, 'for I do not remember to have heard of any one man that spoke Irish, who had not the accent upon his tongue easily discernible to any English ear' (IV, 281). It is also interesting to notice, in view of Swift's own ambivalence about Ireland, that Houyhnhnmland is the only place where Gulliver is an outcast. Here he has no friends as he had in other countries he visited, whatever his size. There is no one to help him to adapt to his new society as there had previously been. He cannot integrate, he cannot eat the Houyhnhnm food or live in their houses, but has to live nearby as though he smelled. Eventually he accepts the ostracism as totally deserved. He must keep his clothes on to hide his nakedness which would ally him to the Yahoos. In Brobdingnag the human skin looked ugly, but now the very possession of human skin is a sign of degeneracy.

The Houyhnhnm regime is totalitarian and contains rigid class distinction. Worse still, their society is divided on racial lines and society falls *naturally* into class divisions:

He made me observe that among the Houyhnhnms, the white, the sorrel, and the iron-grey were not so exactly shaped as the bay, the dapple-grey, and the black; nor born with equal talents of mind, or a capacity to improve them; and therefore continued always in the condition of servants, without ever aspiring to match out of their own race, which in [109] that country would be reckoned monstrous and unnatural (XI, 256).

Family planning is ordained by the state. The Houyhnhnms may produce two children but servant horses may produce three. Marriages are arranged on the basis of friendship and mutual benevolence. Education is state planned and rigid but, in contrast to England at the time, males and females receive more or less the same education. In addition, the Houyhnhnms have slaves.

There are discrepancies in the presentation of the Houyhnhnms, who are in one place presented as gentle and without an army yet elsewhere are shown to have earlier almost wiped out the Yahoos. Perhaps what the Houyhnhnms most fundamentally represent is what we humans aspire to: they are the expression of a human ideal. Perhaps they represent a logical working out of the unacceptable implications of humanity's pretensions to being a rational creature. Both Houyhnhnms and Yahoos lack the capacity for moral choice (since they have no alternative to being as they are) and Swift shows us that what separates man from the animals is precisely this moral choice. It is this which translates our potential for reason into an actual decision to act rationally.

At the end of *Gulliver's Travels* Gulliver leaves Houyhnhnmland and is picked up by a Portugese ship. Its captain, Don Pedro, is described by Gulliver as 'a very courteous and generous person' (XI, 286), and he is often taken as the ideal against whom Gulliver should be measured rather than the extremes of Yahoos and Houyhnhnms. Gulliver has the same problem of adjustment which he found on leaving Brobdingnag, being so deluded that he can only see himself as a Yahoo: but he also exhibits a good deal of the arrogance of the Houyhnhnms in his dismissal of Don Pedro

and his own family. He refuses to accept the nature
[110] of mankind and it takes him a long time to become
rehabilitated. The narrative is supposed to have been
written five years after his return to England and he
has still not completely recuperated from his visit to a
land ruled entirely by reason. There is perhaps hope
for Gulliver at the end of the *Travels*. Swift, however,
leaves matters unconcluded with customary humour.
As Matthew Hodgart says, 'Swift's final defence
against the horors of existence was laughter.'[5]

5

Gulliver's Travels had no noticeable impact on the
political scene of 1726 and added nothing new to the
debate on Ireland's subjugation to England. In the book
Swift reiterated most of the concerns of all his work,
such as his attack on pride and his scepticism about
reason, and used the techniques he used all his
life: the various kinds of irony and the ruthless strip-
ping away of externals to probe the essentials beneath.
The concerns expressed in the book are those of his
eighteenth-century Tory contemporaries; in particular
the rather pessimistic view of the progress of mankind.

It would be rash to attempt to sum up the effect of
the book. Angus Ross writes that 'the total impression
left with the reader is rather a tension between personal
uncertainty and traditional pictures of order, or between rebellious wit and acceptance'.[6] It is this tension
which accounts for the greatness of the book and it is
not too fanciful to recall the creative results of tension
which a later major Anglo-Irish writer and admirer of
Swift discussed and made the underlying motive of so
much of his poetry. W.B. Yeats wrote, 'We make out
of the quarrel with others rhetoric, out of the quarrel
with ourselves, poetry.'

In April 1727 Swift left Ireland for his last visit to
England, calling first at his grandfather's old church at

Goodrich in Herefordshire and then visiting Pope at Twickenham and also Lord Oxford's son. He was ill [111] much of the time, even though he was greatly enjoying meeting old friends, and he intended to visit France for the sake of his health. He felt that he was in England to say goodbye to his friends. In June Bolingbroke advised him not to go to France since it seemed that Walpole would fall from office and the Tories would once again return to power; but even though George I died in June and was succeeded by his apparently pro-Tory son George II, this did not happen. Swift became unhappy, ill and disillusioned: then at the end of August Sheridan wrote that Stella was dying.

So in September Swift set out to Ireland for the last time, only to be held up at Holyhead for a week, where he wrote a bitter poem about his feelings entitled 'Holyhead September 25th 1727'.

Lo here I sit at holy head
With muddy ale and mouldy bread
All christian vittals stink of fish
I'm where my enemies would wish . . .
I never was in haste before
To reach that slavish hateful shore . . .
A passage to the land I hate. (II, 420)

He also wrote 'Ireland', which is another tirade:

Remove me from this land of slaves
Where all are fools and all are knaves
Where every fool and knave is bought
Yet kindly sells himself for nought
Where Whig and Tory fiercely fight
Who's in the wrong, who in the right
And when their country lies at stake
They only fight for fighting sake,
While English sharpers take the pay,
And then stand by to see fair play,
Meantime the Whig is always winner
And for his courage gets — a dinner. (II, 421)

A Poisoned Rat in a Hole

1

When Swift arrived in Dublin he found Stella still alive. Before leaving England he had written the last of his birthday poems and in it he accepted her impending death. This last poem is the nearest he ever came to a love poem. He accepts the reality of her situation and is not concerned to draw a veil of illusion over the fact 'that you are sick, and I grown old'. So the poem opens on a note of bravado:

> This day, whate'er the fates decree,
> Shall still be kept with joy by me. (II, 763)

The poem both portrays an awareness of death and is a celebration of the past friendship of the two:

> Say, Stella, feel you no content,
> Reflecting on a life well spent? (II, 764)

He appears at her bedside as priest-healer and the poem is virtually a straightforward praise of her friendship expressed in the close language of that friendship while he tries to prepare her to face death. It is an essentially Christian poem focused on the virtues of charity and the corporal works of mercy. He also argues the superiority of Stella's fortitude over its pagan stoical counterparts. The poem ends movingly:

> O then, whatever Heaven intends,
> Take pity on your pitying friends;
> Nor let your ills affect your mind,
> To fancy they can be unkind.

Me, surely me, you ought to spare,
Who gladly would your sufferings share;
Or give my scrap of life to you,
And think it far beneath your due;
You, to whose care so oft I owe,
That I'm alive to tell you so. (II, 766)

In October he wrote to Pope, in effect saying good-bye to him, 'You are the best and kindest friend in the world . . . I have often wished that God Almighty would be so easy to the weakness of mankind, as to let old friends be acquainted in another state; and if I were to write an Utopia for heaven, that would be one of my schemes. This wildness you must allow for, because I am giddy and deaf' (iii, 242).

Stella died on Sunday 28 January 1728 in the early evening. Swift was entertaining at the Deanery when he heard the news: 'about eight o'clock at night a servant brought me a note, with an account of the death of the truest, most virtuous, and valuable friend, that I, or perhaps any other person, ever was blessed with' (V, 227). Once his visitors had left at about eleven o'clock he started to write down his feelings in *On the Death of Mrs Johnson*. The next day he wrote, 'My head aches and I can write no more' (V, 229). On the following evening she was buried in St Patrick's and he continued the diary: 'This is the night of the funeral, which my sickness will not suffer me to attend' (V, 229). He had moved into another room to avoid seeing the light of the church. In his account of Stella he gives the events of her life, stressing the quality of her mind and the part she played in giving him advice and criticism, 'Never was so happy a conjunction of civility, freedom, easiness and sincerity' (V, 228-9). He tells of her bravery in confronting a robber and mortality wounding him with a pistol. He praises her as 'but little versed in the common topics

of female chat; scandal, censure, and detraction,
[114] never came out of her mouth' (V, 230) and delineates
her qualities at great length, presenting her as a
paragon of virtue, but a very likeable paragon. Stella
left her money to Dr Steevens's Hospital, which is
coincidentally next door to the hospital Swift later
founded. His account is so objective and dispassionate
that there is no real indication of his own emotions
towards her. It is interesting to consider his self-
control in holding his own feelings at bay immediately
after her death by writing this paean of praise for his
very old dear friend. We have little correspondence
between Swift and Stella. One theory is that Bishop
Berkeley, the philosopher and old friend of Swift,
as one of Stella's executors perhaps disposed of the
letters in order to clear Swift. It is also thought that
Swift himself may have destroyed her letters to him.

He continued to be active for a decade after Stella's
death, keeping his feelings under control by sustained
energy. He wrote pamphlets and some of his most
vigorous poetry, and continued to work for the
alleviation of the conditions around him in Ireland.
He continued to complain of his imprisonment in
Ireland and in 1730 wrote that unless rescued from
Ireland he would die there 'like a poisoned rat in a
hole' (iii, 383). As always, his friends sustained him.
In Ireland he often visited the Grattans at Belcamp;
at the Grange near Dublin there was Lady Acheson's
mother; Sheridan was master of the free school in
Cavan and Swift stayed frequently with him. Until his
death in October 1738 Sheridan was Swift's closest
friend and they often exchanged humorous punning
poems in Latin and English or in a mixture of both.
Delany often entertained at his Villa Delville in North
Dublin and Swift also paid occasional visits to Lord
and Lady Howth at Howth Castle. His favourite spot,
however, was Market Hill (now Gosford Castle) near

Armagh, where his friends Sir Arthur and Lady Acheson frequently entertained him. In 1728 he [115] stayed six months with them as well as in the summers of 1729 and 1730, writing some of his most personal poetry around incidents there. These are light-hearted poems on quite trivial subjects, but written to please his hosts and presumably as an act of gratitude for hospitality. One of the longer Market Hill poems was 'A panegyric on the Dean in the person of a lady from the North', where Swift pays himself an ironic tribute through the alleged comments of Lady Acheson. The poem begins on a fairly serious note:

> Resolved my gratitude to show,
> Thrice reverend Dean for all I owe;
> Too long I have my thanks delayed,
> Your favours left too long unpaid.
> But now in all our sex's name,
> My artless muse shall sing your fame. (III, 887)

However, the Lady goes on to discuss the building of two temples to the goddess Cloacina (the Latin word for 'sewer') and Swift writes a burlesque account of the building of two privies at Market Hill:

> Two temples of magnific size,
> Attract the curious traveller's eyes,
> That might be envied by the Greeks,
> Raised up by you in twenty weeks.
> Here gentle goddess Cloacine
> Receives all offerings at her shrine,
> In sep'rate cells the he's and she's
> Here pay their vows with bended knees:
> (For 'tis prophane when sexes mingle,
> And every nymph must enter single,
> And when she feels an inward motion,
> Comes filled with reverence and devotion.)
> The bashful maid, to hide her blush,

Shall creep no more behind a bush,
Here unobserved, she boldly goes,
As who should say, to pluck a rose. (III, 893)

In addition to these old and new friends in Ireland, Swift kept up a lively correspondence with friends in England. Chief among these were Lady Betty Germain, and Charles Ford, who moved there in 1732. He also wrote regularly to Gay, who died at the end of 1732, Arbuthnot, who died in 1735 ('I am going out of this troublesome world; and you, among the rest of my friends, shall have my last prayers and good wishes') and Bolingbroke, who outlived Swift and died in 1751. Swift's most valued friend during the last years of his life was Pope and their correspondence was prolific until Swift lost his memory in 1740. So Swift kept contact with his friends in England through his massive correspondence. His facility at letter writing has never been fully acknowledged, yet he is perhaps as great a letter writer as Horace Walpole. The scope of the letters ranges from the short and humorous to great formal letters. There are letters to Vanessa and Stella full of emotion and affection and brilliant exercises in linguistic artistry, such as the letter to Sheridan containing 160 words ending in '-ling' in reply to Sheridan's thirteen (iv, 346-8).

However, although Swift was able to find temporary escape in social life and in writing, he was growing progressively more gloomy so that his letters up to 1737 are filled with references to his ill health and to the bad conditions in Ireland. Ireland was 'a mass of beggars, thieves, oppressors, fools and knaves' (iv, 249). He was sick of the world, sick of age and disease, 'the last of which I am never wholly without' (iv, 303), and wrote that 'I live in a nation of slaves, who sell themselves for nothing' (iv, 303). It is always difficult to know how seriously these pronouncements should be taken, since Swift was prone to couch his letters in somewhat exaggerated language.

On 11 May 1728 the first issue of the *Intelligencer* appeared. It was a weekly periodical which Sheridan and Swift used as a vehicle for the discussion of Irish problems and for attacks on personal enemies, especially Richard Tighe. The *Intelligencer* also contained an interesting essay on Gay's *Beggar's Opera*, which was first staged in 1728 and which Swift very much approved of. He discusses satire in this essay, writing of the two aims of satire as personal satisfaction ('laughing with a few friends in a corner') and public spirit ('to mend the world') (XII, 34). He continues with his customary irony, 'My reason for mentioning courts, and ministers, (whom I never think on, but with the most profound veneration) is because an opinion obtains that in the "Beggar's Opera" there appears to be some reflection upon courtiers and statesmen, whereof I am by no means a judge' (XII, 34). One reason for Swift's approval of *The Beggar's Opera* was that he shared with his friends a dislike of the upstart Italian opera:

> This comedy likewise exposes with great justice that unnatural taste for Italian music among us, which is wholly unsuitable to our northern climate and the genius of the people, whereby we are overrun with Italian effeminacy and Italian non-sense. An old gentleman said to me that many years ago when the practice of an unnatural vice grew so frequent in London that many were prosecuted for it, he was sure it would be a fore-runner of Italian operas and singers, and then we should want nothing but stabbing or poisoning to make us perfect Italians. (XII, 36-7).

In addition, the *Intelligencer* took up familiar views about Ireland which Swift had already put forward,

and No. 19, which is from a Northern Irish country
[118] gentleman to the Drapier, deals with the coinage
again ('I may venture that Ireland is the first imperial
kingdom since Nimrod which ever wanted power to
coin their own money') (XII, 57), asserts that many
people are emigrating and compares the Irish to Red
Indians: '. . . the Indians enjoy the product of their
own land, whereas the better half of ours is sent away,
without so much as a recompense in bugles or glass in
return' (XII, 58). But the work proved too much for
Sheridan and Swift alone and the *Intelligencer* ran
for only nineteen issues.

2

Swift's chief concern in the last years of the decade,
as it had been earlier, was with the state of Ireland.
In sermons and pamphlets he wrote about England's
responsibility for Ireland's misery. These were years
of want and hardship in Ireland as we see in his letter
to Pope in 1729, 'there have been three terrible years
dearth of corn, and every place strewed with
beggars . . .' (iii, 341). Swift had, with complete
honesty, always argued that the Irish themselves
hardly helped matters:

> Imagine a nation the two thirds of whose revenues
> are spent out of it and who are not permitted to
> trade with the other third, and where the pride of
> the women will not suffer them to wear their own
> manufactures even where they excel what comes
> from abroad. This is the true state of Ireland in a
> very few words. These evils operate more every day
> and the kingdom is absolutely undone as I have been
> telling it often in print these ten years past (iii, 341).

Of the many papers which Swift wrote on the condition of Ireland there are two important ones from

1728 and from 1729, when he was given the freedom of the City of Dublin. The first is *A Short View of the* [119] *State of Ireland*, which obviously echoed Edmund Spenser's *View of the Present State of Ireland* (1595-7) and the second is the well-known *Modest Proposal.*

Written and published towards the end of 1728, the pamphlet *A Short View* summarises the disadvantages under which Ireland suffered at the time and reinforces the argument that these were mainly due to England's jealousy and stupid indifference. Swift, however, once again made clear his habitual point that the people of Ireland were themselves to blame, though to a much lesser degree. The pamphlet was occasioned by the poor harvest of 1727, which had brought starvation to hundreds of peasants and had driven thousands from their homes. In 1728 the country was again threatened with famine since the lack of grain had forced many farmers to harvest their potatoes two months earlier than usual, and once this supply had been used up there would have been no food left. The pamphlet enumerates some fourteen causes of a nation's prosperity and proceeds to show why it is that these causes either do not exist in Ireland or else have been prevented from operating. He invites the 'worthy commissioners who come from England' to travel round the thriving country and report back with enthusiasm. But this is extremely unlikely because although the country is potentially fruitful, everywhere there is desolation and poverty: 'These indeed may be comfortable sights to an English spectator, who comes for a short time only to learn the language and returns back to his own country, whither he finds all our wealth transmitted' (XII, 10-11). The pamphlet demonstrates that what in most countries would be evidence of wealth, was in Ireland simply proof of the country's poverty. In Ireland, for example, the high cost of living was the

result not of prosperity but of landlords who increas-
[120] ed rents so that tenants had to raise the price of cattle
and grain with the result that the deceptive inflation
spread to all sections of the national economy.

The full title of the second pamphlet is *A Modest
Proposal for preventing the children of poor people
from being a burthen to their parents or country, and
for making them beneficial to the public.* It represents
the culmination of ten years of warning the people
of Ireland and trying to incite them to action. It has
certainly achieved one of its purposes over the years:
causing physical revulsion as a means of bringing
home to people the appalling state of Ireland in 1729.
What people mostly remember is the central suggestion
that children should be fattened up for market and
then sold and eaten.

The pamphlet continues the arguments put forward
in Swift's other writings on Ireland, but he also writes
here in protest against the contemporary maxim
that 'people are the riches of a nation'. In Ireland,
Swift realised, populousness was *not* a virtue but a
liability. However, his chief concern is for Ireland
to have not fewer people but more opportunities. At
the time he wrote the *Proposal* there were many
pamphlets available dealing with population and
poverty and the 'projector', whose guise he dons for
this work, sounds like yet another political mathematician coming forward with his schemes for solving
Ireland's problems. These projects had flourished
since the formation of the Royal Society in 1662
and Swift had already had great fun with their
schemes and projects in *Gulliver's Travels.*

The projector begins with a matter-of-fact description of the misery of Ireland with its hordes of beggars
and their attendant children all in rags. He proceeds
briskly to suggest that anyone who could 'find out a
fair, cheap and easy method of making these children

sound, useful members of the commonwealth would deserve so well of the public as to have his statue set [121] up for a preserver of the nation' (XII, 109). This projector plans to outdo his rivals and (like Herod before him) include 'the whole number of infants at a certain age' (XII, 110). He is well versed in Swift's rhetorical ploys: exaggeration ('having turned my thoughts for many years') (XII, 110), impressive mathematics which are not always accurate ('I calculate there may be about two hundred thousand couple whose wives are breeders, from which number I subtract thirty thousand couples . . .') (XII, 110), and affected knowledge ('I have been informed by a principal gentleman in the county of Cavan') (XII, 111). Very subtly Swift has the projector reveal his own attitude to human beings, and if we are not careful we may miss the irony and continue to nod along in agreement: 'it is true that a child, just dropped from its dam . . .' (XII, 110). Here is the language of the truly objective theoretician, treating humans as though they were breeding cattle. In innocent enthusiasm the projector argues that his scheme will benefit everyone (except the children) financially and will also prevent other crimes, which may or may not have been prevalent at the time, such as the murder by parents of children born and not yet born to save money, which, the Projector argues, 'would move tears and pity in the most savage and inhuman breast' (XII, 110) (but not in *human* hearts presumably, since they are harder still).

The projector then indulges in a good deal of computation to decide how many children there are and then proposes his project 'humbly', hoping that it 'will not be liable to the least objection' (XII, 111). His project 'that a young healthy child well nursed is at a year old a most delicious, nourishing and wholesome food, whether stewed, roasted, baked or boiled, and I make no doubt that it will equally [122] serve in a fricasee or a ragout' (XII, 111), is based on the fake assurance of a 'very knowing American' of his acquaintance in London (America was at the time reputed to be inhabited by cannibals and London was an appropriate place to meet those who treat humans as cattle). The projector then continues with his scheme, which is really macabre, but otherwise 'reasonable' if the reader has been suitably lulled by Swift's skill: 'A child will make two dishes at an entertainment for friends, and when the family dines alone, the fore or hind quarters will make a reasonable dish, and seasoned with a little pepper or salt will be very good boiled on the fourth day, especially in winter' (XII, 112). Then Swift makes the first forceful point which shows where the *Proposal* is really aimed, 'I grant this food will be somewhat dear, and therefore very proper for land-lords, who as they have already devoured most of the parents, seem to have the best title to the children' (XII, 112). After a relentless succession of arguments in favour of his proposal, the projector then uses another of Swift's rhetorical methods: to pretend not to accept all the consequences, and in this case any possible accusation of cruelty. Before he finishes clinching his proposals the projector lets the mask slip again in giving away his real intention: 'But I am not in the least pain upon that matter, because it is very well known, that they are every day dying and rotting, by cold and famine and filth and vermin as fast as can be reasonably expected' (XII, 114). The horror behind that 'reasonably' may not have been noticed by all Swift's readers.

Then the projector lists six advantages resulting from his modest proposal: there would be a reduction in the number of Catholics in Ireland (not only 'the principal breeders of the nation' but politically suspect), poorer tenants would have something valuable at last (something which could be seized if they [123] got behind with the rent), there would be an increase in Ireland's financial stock and the introduction of a new dish, 'constant breeders' would be relieved of looking after their children after the first year, tavern custom would increase, a great inducement to marriage would follow as well as an increase in 'the care and tenderness of mothers towards their children . . .' (XII, 115) — the bitterest irony.

Finally, with great skill, Swift makes his projector say 'let no man talk to me of other expedients' (XII, 116), and he appears to dismiss as unworkable ten ways of solving Ireland's ills, all of which have been proposed for years by him and other patriots (such as taxing absentees and buying only Irish goods). Here is where the irony strikes home. The projector then aims a discreet blow at England: 'We can incur no danger of disobliging England. For this kind of commodity will not bear exportation, the flesh being of too tender a consistency to admit a long continuance in salt, although perhaps I could name a country, which would be glad to eat up our whole nation without it' (XII, 117). He concludes with a strongly worded personal disclaimer that he cannot benefit from the scheme as his youngest child is nine and his wife past child-bearing.

There can be no more savage and effective satire in the English language.

3

In 1720 Swift had written that 'the two principal branches of preaching are first to tell the people what is their duty; and then to convince them that it is so' (IX, 70). Some time during the following decade he preached his sermon *Causes of the Wretched Condition of Ireland.* Here he summarised the causes of Ireland's [124] poverty, all of which he treated elsewhere. The two chief causes of Ireland's misery are identified as in the area of trade (that is, the crippling mercantile laws imposed by England, which have led the Irish to 'become as hewers of wood and drawers of water to our rigorous neighbours') (IX, 200), and absentee-ism, whereby absentees 'draw out the very vitals of their mother kingdom' (IX, 200). In *A Proposal for the Universal Use of Irish Manufacture* he had told the fable of Arachne and Pallas, and, referring to England, had concluded the fable by saying that 'for the greatest part of our bowels and vitals is extracted without allowing us the liberty of spinning and weaving them' (IX, 18).

The faults of the Irish are, firstly, monstrous pride and vanity, 'priding themselves to wear nothing but what comes from abroad' (IX, 200). Here Swift is indulging in his habitual exaggeration and suggesting that the Irish do the opposite to what he proposed in *Universal Use* and elsewhere. He had persistently tried to persuade the Irish of the folly of importing clothes from England when they could produce their own, and was forever championing the weavers and kindred indigenous trades. The second fault is great luxury in the way money is spent, and the third is that the native Irish are 'from their infancy so given up to idleness and sloth that they often choose to beg or steal rather than support themselves with their own labour; they marry without the least view or thought of being able to make any provision for their families' (IX, 200). Finally, there is 'the Egyptian bondage of cruel, oppressing, covetous landlords' (IX, 201). All these causes, Swift suggests, are not the main reasons and if he had 'leisure or liberty to lay it before you' (IX, 202) he would have provided even more evidence.

In addition, he urged the increased building of charity schools and was a member of the Board of the Dublin Workhouse and Foundling Society. He also dealt with one of his favourite subjects: identifying bona fide beggars by their wearing badges to show which parishes they belonged to. He followed this up later with a pamphlet in 1737 entitled *A Proposal for giving Badges to the Beggars in all the Parishes of Dublin*. It is important to stress the impact which Swift made on contemporary Dublin. His charity was outstanding and there are many stories of his secret donations to the poor and suffering of all denominations. He was very zealous in his church activity, restored weekly communion to the Cathedral (almost alone in Dublin), came to church every morning and attended the evening anthem. As his friend Delany summed him up: 'He lived a blessing, he died a benefactor, and his name will ever live an honour of Ireland.'[1]

Above all, Swift was concerned to force the Irish to act for themselves. He added practical recommendations to theoretical speculation: taxing absentee landlords, encouraging Irish manufacture, making the Irish buy Irish goods, import controls, improving manufacturing goods and also land and agriculture. And he had little or no success in practical achievement. It was not only the economic situation of Ireland which dismayed him but the physical conditions:

A bare face of nature without houses or plantations; filthy cabins, miserable, tattered, half-starved creatures, scarce in human shape; one insolent ignorant oppressive squire to be found in twenty miles riding; a parish church to be found only in a summer day's journey . . . a bog of fifteen miles round; every meadow a slough, and every hill a mixture of rock, heath and marsh . . . There is not an acre of land in Ireland turned to half its

advantage; yet it is better improved than the people;
and all these evils are effects of English tyranny . . .'
(iv, 34).

He also described Ireland in a letter of 1732 where he wrote that the English ought to be 'ashamed of the reproaches they cast on the ignorance, the dullness and the want of courage in the Irish natives; those defects . . . arising only from the poverty and slavery they suffer from their inhuman neighbours . . . the millions of oppressions they lie under . . . have been enough to damage the best spirits under the sun' (iv, 51).

Swift became involved in Irish church politics in the early thirties. He attacked the Irish bishops, who proposed bills which he felt were designed to worsen the conditions of country clergy, celebrating the rejection of the bills in verse:

Our bishops puffed up with wealth and with pride,
To hell on the backs of the clergy would ride;
They mounted and laboured with whip and with spur
In vain – for the devil a person would stir. (III, 804)

The next religious battle was yet another attack on the Test Act and Swift issued a series of pamphlets that took up again the attacks on Dissenters and their schemes which he had not made since the pamphlets of 1709. Parliament met soon after in October 1733 and rejected a repeal of the Test. Then he crossed swords with Richard Bettesworth, Serjeant-at-Law and a member of parliament, whom he pursued as vigorously as he had other Irish enemies such as Dean Smedley, Richard Tighe and Lord Allen:

Thus at the Bar that booby Bettesworth,
Though half a crown o'erpays his sweat's worth;
(III, 812)

When Bettesworth asked Swift if he had written the

poem, Swift replied: 'Mr Bettesworth, I was in my youth acquainted with great lawyers, who, knowing my disposition to satire, advised me, that if any scoundrel or blockhead whom I had lampooned should ask, Are you the author of this page? I should tell him that I was not the author, and therefore I tell you, Mr Bettesworth, that I am not the author of these lines.'[2] Bettesworth threatened to cut off his ears and went in search of him, armed with a sharp knife and accompanied by a footman and several thugs. Swift's account was widely read: 'When he began to grow over-warm and eloquent I called in the gentleman of the house from the room adjoining and the Serjeant, going on with less turbulence, went away' (iv, 220). Swift's neighbours in the Liberty of St Patrick's passed a resolution to defend his life and limbs and, in his usual fashion, he prolonged the attack on Bettesworth with verses which included 'The Yahoo's overthrow':

Jolly boys of St Kevan's, St Patrick's, Donore,
And Smithfield, I'll tell you, if not told before,
How Bettesworth, that booby, and scoundrel in grain,
Hath insulted us all by insulting the Dean.
Knock him down, down, down, knock him down.

(III, 814)

Swift continued to involve himself in Irish politics in minor skirmishes until 1736 when landowners in Parliament tried to pass a bill which would enable them to avoid certain tithes. As a result, he produced one of his greatest satires, 'The Legion Club', which proposed the dissolution of the Irish Parliament (the 'Legion Club') and the confinement of its members as madmen. The source for the poem is the fifth chapter of St Mark's Gospel, where Christ exorcises the devils who have taken possession of the Gadarene madmen and transfers them to swine. The spirit tells

Christ, 'My name is Legion, for we are many.' It was [128] fashionable to visit lunatic asylums at the time and there is in the poem the air of curiosity of a visit to Bedlam:

> As I strole the City, oft I
> Spy a building large and lofty,
> Not a bow-shot from the College,
> Half the globe from sense and knowledge.
> By the prudent architect
> Placed against the church direct;
> Making good my grandame's jest,
> *Near the church* — you know the rest
> [i.e. 'far from God']
> Tell us what this pile contains:
> Many a head that holds no brains.
> These demoniacs let me dub
> With the name of Legion Club. (III, 829)

The poem gives Swift the chance to attack all his enemies in libellous fashion. The speaker of the poem refers to Swift:

> Yet should Swift endow the schools
> For his lunatics and fools. (III, 830)

Swift attacked individual members of parliament:

> In the porch Briareus stands,
> Shows a bribe in all his hands:
> Briareus, the Secretary,
> But we mortals call him Cary . . . (III, 833)
> Who is that hell-featured brawler,
> Is it Satan? No, 'tis Waller . . . (III, 834)
> Keeper, yon old dotart smoke,
> Sweetly snoring in his cloak.
> Who is he? 'Tis humdrum Wynne,
> Half encompassed by his kin. (III, 836)

The atmosphere of the poem reminds the reader of a

painting by Hogarth, whom Swift actually invokes:

> How I want thee, humorous Hogart
> Thou I hear, a pleasant rogue art;
> Were but you and I acquainted,
> Every monster should be painted;
> You should try your graving tools
> On this odious group of fools;
> Draw the beasts as I describe 'em
> Form their features, while I gibe them;
> Draw them like, for I assure you,
> You will need no caricatura;
> Draw them so that we may trace
> All the soul in every face. (III, 839)

At the end of the wild journey, made more surrealistic by a verse style which gives the poem a wild and apparently uncontrolled vividness, the speaker seems to retire in despair and consigns them all to their 'god':

> Keeper, I have seen enough,
> Taking then a pinch of snuff;
> I concluded, looking round 'em,
> May their god, the Devil, confound 'em.
>
> (III, 839)

There are many traditional anecdotes about Swift dating from this time in Dublin and from many years afterwards. He is, for example, traditionally connected with Carolan, the last of the great harpers, one of whose patrons was Swift's friend Delany. Presumably Carolan's patrons must have understood Irish. It is not certain that Swift and Carolan met, but Carolan composed music for Hugh MacGauran's humorous poem, 'Pléaráca na Ruarcach', the only Gaelic poem that Swift translated (as 'The description of an Irish feast'). We do not certainly know how far Swift knew Gaelic, but lecturers in the subject were certainly employed at Trinity College, and a knowledge of the [130] language was widespread among the Protestant Anglo-Irish. Because of his popularity in Dublin there grew up many stories and anecdotes about 'the Dane' of St Patrick's, his eccentricities and his servant, often called Jack, who, in the stories, usually got the better of his master.

4

As well as involving himself in Irish politics and religious affairs Swift had other interests. In the early autumn of 1731 he wrote to Gay that he had retired to the country with two 'great works' in hand, one of which was 'to reduce the whole politness, wit, humour and style of England into a short system for the use of all persons of quality, and particularly the maids of honour' (iii, 493), the other was to be a 'Whole Duty of Servants'. The first of these was *A Complete Collection of General and Ingenious Conversation, According to the Most Polite Mode and Method Now used at Court, and the Best Companies of England*, which was published in 1738 and is usually referred to as *Polite Conversation*. Swift had begun this in 1704 and it appeared as the work of Simon Wagstaff Esq., who had apparently spent his life attending the gatherings of genteel folk in order to write down their conversation, which he now offered to the public in the form of dialogue masquerading as models of wit and repartee. They are, as one would expect, completely commonplace and cliché-ridden. The second of these handbooks was *Directions to Servants*, not published until shortly after his death in 1745. He worked on it from time to time between 1730 and 1740 and one of his 'Directions to the Footman' will give the flavour: 'Take off the largest dishes and set them on with one hand, to show the ladies your vigour and strength of back; but always do it between two ladies, that if the dish happens to slip, [131] the soup or sauce may fall on their clothes and not daub the floor' (XIII, 35).

5

The thirties were also years of prolific poetic achievement for Swift and they are marked especially by the 'scatological' poems. There has been considerable discussion about these poems. Until recently they were seen as an embarrassment and many critics recoiled from them, accusing Swift of a morbid obsession with excrement and bodily functions. John Middleton Murry wrote of Swift's 'excremental vision' and Aldous Huxley felt that a disturbance of the genital function caused Swift's unusual relations with Stella and Vanessa. Other critics have 'excused' him on the grounds of diminished responsibility and even employed psychiatric methods to give explanations. One writer, in a significantly titled 'Neurotic traits of Jonathan Swift', wrote of Swift as 'a neurotic who exhibited psychosexual infantilism, with a particular showing of coprophilia, associated with misogyny, misanthropy, mysophilia and mysophobia' (15, 34). Certainly these poems are powerful and it is possible to take lines out of context which might cause revulsion. It is true that Swift does dwell in great detail on many unpleasant features of dress, body, and bodily functions. At the end of 'A Beautiful Young Nymph going to Bed' there is little doubt that 'who sees will spew; who smells be poisoned'. What he found in Celia's dressing room 'turned poor Strephon's bowels', as it did those of the reader. Swift insists on his survey and insists that no dirty washing is left unturned. However, these poems naturally complement the concerns he expresses in *Gulliver's*

Travels and in much of his other writing; and they are [132] certainly not a misanthrope's momentary vision of hell. Nor are they anti-feminine diatribes, as has been argued, since the men in the poems are as badly mauled as the women, who are, it needs to be said, usually treated with compassion; the 'beautiful young nymph', for example, is seen as preyed upon.

Swift had written several scatological poems before the 1730s, in particular his three burlesques of the 'progress' poem popular in his day: 'Phyllis, or the Progress of Love' and 'The Progress of Beauty' in 1719 and 'The Progress of Marriage' in 1722. Since he was the sworn enemy of the typical love poem, which contained, he felt, so much self-deception, these poems attack the literary conventions of romanticising physical beauty and the general tendency to confuse physical attraction with moral excellence. They also share with the later poems the common theme of the disparity between appearance and reality. In 'The Lady's Dressing Room' (1730) the hero Strephon loves the image he has created of his beloved Celia and in examining the secrets of her dressing room finds all the unpleasant aspects of her toilet preparations. Here one remembers the stripped maids of honour in Brobdingnag.

In 1731 Swift wrote his three scatological poems, 'A Beautiful Young Nymph going to bed', 'Strephon and Chloe' and 'Cassinus and Peter', which continue the same theme. The first describes the physical disintegration of the pathetic prostitute Corinna as she prepares for bed. The poem displays the features typical of these poems: a frankness that is too much for many readers, a stubborn realism, an irreverence for the deceptions of romantic conventions in poetry, an impatience with false delicacy and a considerable comic sense.

'Strephon and Chloe' continues the lesson which the

reader learns more quickly than the two lovers themselves, who need the whole poem before:

> How great a change! how quickly made!
> They learn to call a spade, a spade. (II, 590)

For Swift, true marriage is based on more permanent values (the mind and the heart) and he argues that if only Strephon had seen Chloe as human like himself then his experiences would have been different, 'since beauty scare endures a day'. However, Strephon insisted on thinking of Chloe as a goddess:

> While she a goddess dyed in grain
> Was unsusceptible of stain:
> And, Venus-like, her fragrant skin
> Exhaled Ambrosia from within:
> Can such a deity endure
> A moral human touch impure? (II, 586)

Strephon is shattered when she comes down to earth to relieve herself: Can Chloe, heavenly Chloe piss? (II, 589)

'Cassinus and Peter' is largely a discussion between two undergraduates who pride themselves on the fineness of their sensibilities in literary and emotional criticism. Their wit and learning are derived from the romances of which they are devotees. Peter visits Cassinus, who sits in a state of total disarray not dissimilar to that of the lady's dressing room or the bedroom of the beautiful young nymph. In what is certainly a parody of the affected diction of the pastoral poet, Cassinus behaves like a love-sick swain. But what has happened to him is worse than the death of his nymph Caelia, worse than if she were a whore, worse than if she had the pox: for 'Caelia, Caelia Caelia shits' (II, 597). Cassinus has learnt one of the lessons which Swift wants to impart to his readers:

Oh Peter! Beauty's but a varnish,
Which time and accidents will tarnish. (II, 595)

This is a major preoccupation in these poems: the varnish of Celia's beauty in 'The Progress of Beauty', the false exterior of the lady's dressing room, the illusion with which Strephon surrounds Chloe. Swift's life was haunted by the impermanence of events. Denis Donoghue sums up the intention of these poems: 'The motto of these poems is: live with illusion, but know that you are being deceived; beguile yourself with the image before you, but know that it is a pleasant fiction' (35, 209). Cassinus and the other beaux of these poems are victims of their own imaginations and fancies. For Swift it was truly Christian to recognise oneself with one's imperfect nature. These poems are further evidence of Swift's total honesty pursued to limits which many readers refuse to follow. He insists throughout his work on cutting through man's delusions and his refusal to look below the surface, and on making man accept how things really are.

We have already seen that one of his main concerns in these poems is the gap between appearance and reality. The destroying of man's illusions often leads him towards madness. Gulliver becomes mad and Swift himself became increasingly, perhaps even morbidly, obsessed with madness. His Uncle Godwin died in madness and, like Johnson later, Swift felt himself menaced by insanity. Yeats followed the nineteenth-century historian Lecky in suggesting that dread of madness even caused Swift to fight shy of marriage and procreation. But Swift could joke about his illness and in 'Verses on the Death of Dr Swift' he wrote:

That old vertigo in his head,
Will never leave him till he's dead:

Besides, his memory decays,
He recollects not what he says;   [135]
He cannot call his friends to mind;
Forgets the place where last he dined:
Plies you with stories o'er and o'er,
He told them fifty times before. (II, 556)

Swift's ultimate vision of madness was 'The Legion Club', but 'The Lady's Dressing Room' and the other scatological poems qualify as madmen. In addition, He exhibited the contemporary distrust of the imagination, which led to the attack on 'enthusiasm' in religious affairs, but he was not so much an enemy of imagination as distrustful of its potentially anarchic nature. He wrote about fools and madmen. The philosopher Locke had stated that one was *born* a fool but one *became* mad. Madmen were considered to be those who joined things together incorrectly, mistaking them for truth. So the heroes of the scatological poems qualify as madmen. In addition, a failure to face reality leads to madness. This is a further outward sign of the characters in these poems: madness or obsession comes when the fantasy world collapses, as Gulliver's did.

Even greater than these poems are the 'Verses on the Death of Dr. Swift' composed in 1731. 'When I was of your age,' Swift wrote to Pope when the latter was forty-five, 'I thought every day of death, but now [at sixty-six], every minute.' (iv, 152) Swift constantly meditated on death from an early age (and this is not surprising when one considers the severe pain he was in from time to time from Ménière's disease). This preoccupation with death is much in line with earlier writers of the seventeenth-century such as John Donne and Sir Thomas Browne.

The 'Verses' are the culmination of Swift's poems about himself and they are closely connected with the majority of the poems about Stella. The poem [136] (fittingly for a poem of Swift's old age) is also about the final inescapable physical condition of human existence: the necessity of dying. In this often light-hearted poem Swift discusses his own death and the hypothetical reaction to it from friends and enemies. It begins with a maxim by the French moralist La Rochefoucauld, whose realistic (some would say cynical) view of life he so much admired, 'in the adversity of our best friends we find something that does not displease us'. He then applies the maxim to a particular case and imagines the attitudes of his friends to his own death. Then, in the last section of the poem, he takes on the most difficult task of assessing his own achievements. As well as this summing-up and re-statement of what he has tried to do, he celebrates his friends in the poem in a way which anticipates and may have influenced Yeats's celebration, for example, of Robert Gregory in his 'In Memory of Major Robert Gregory'.

There is a good deal of controversy about the 'Verses' and in particular about the last part. Swift is in satiric vein when he speculates on the future prospects of his work:

> Now Curl his shop from rubbish drains;
> Three genuine tomes of Swift's remains.
> And then to make them pass the glibber,
> Revised by Tibbalds, Moore and Cibber.

(II, 560-1)

The poem contains a defence of Swift's satiric method: he claims to correct vice, to direct his attacks at general classes and not individuals and never to ridicule natural deformities (unlike some who attacked his friend Pope):

> "Perhaps I may allow, the Dean
> "Had too much satire in his vein;

"And seemed determined not to starve it,
"Because no age could more deserve it.   [137]
"Yet malice never was his aim,
"He lashed the vice but spared the name.
"No individual could resent,
"Where thousands equally were meant.
"His satire points at no defect,
"But what all mortals may correct.
"For he abhorred that senseless tribe,
"Who calls it humour when they jibe:
"He spared a hump or crooked nose,
"Whose owners set not up for beaux.
"True genuine dullness moved his pity,
"Unless it offered to be witty." (II, 571-2)

He also manages to remind the reader of his own
battles for Ireland's freedom:

"Fair Liberty was all his cry;
"For her he stood prepared to die;
"For her he boldly stood alone;
"For her he oft exposed his own.
"Two kingdoms, just as factions led,
"Had set a price upon his head;
"But not a traitor could be found,
"To sell him for six hundred pound." (II, 566-7)

There is some brilliant mimicry of the social scene,
which he had portrayed in some of his earliest society
poetry:

My female friends, whose tender hearts
Have better learned to act their parts
Receive the news in doleful dumps,
"The Dean is dead, (and what is Trumps?)
"The Lord have mercy on his soul,
"(Ladies, I'll venture for the vole.)
"Six deans they say must bear the pall,
"(I wish I knew what king to call.) (II, 562)

Swift wrote to Pope in May 1735 'I never am a day without frequent terrors of a fit of giddiness; my head is never well, and I cannot walk after night-fall. My memory is going fast, my spirits are sunk nine parts in ten' (iv, 333). The letter continues in similar vein. In 1937 he wrote, 'I have not one rag of memory left, and my friends have all forsaken me' (v, 28). His friends Gay and Arbuthnot and Orrery had all died and in 1731 he had become estranged from Knightley Chetwode. In 1732 he told Arbuthnot, 'like Caesar I will be one of the first here rather than the last among you'. In 1738 he described his endless activity: 'I seldom walk less than four miles, sometimes six, eight, ten or more, never beyond my own limits; or if it rains I walk as much through the house, up and down stairs' (v, 118). In August 1738 he wrote a sad letter to Pope and Bolingbroke: 'I desire you will look upon me as a man worn with years, and sunk by public as well as personal vexations. I have entirely lost my memory, uncapable of conversation by a cruel deafness, which has lasted almost a year, and I despair of any cure' (v, 119). Some years before he had said to a friend when looking at an elm tree withered and decayed in its upper branches, 'I shall be like that tree: I shall die at the top.'[3]

In May 1740 he made his will, leaving most of his fortune to build and endow 'an hospital large enough for the reception of as many idiots and lunatics as the annual income of the said lands and worldly substance shall be sufficient to maintain; and I desire that the said hospital may be called St Patrick's Hospital' (XIII, 150). It is now sometimes called 'Swift's':

> He gave the little wealth he had
> To build a house for fools and mad. (II, 572)

He left an annuity to Rebecca Dingley and various personal treasures to friends. [139]

On 12 August 1742 a commission 'de lunatico inquirendo' was issued after a petition by two of Swift's friends, and five days later the commissioners found him of unsound mind and memory and incapable of taking care of himself or his possessionns. He was entrusted to the care of the Reverend John Lyon. In October 1742 he was incapacitated by a stroke. One night his left eye swelled up and large boils appeared on his arms and body. His cousin, Mrs Whiteway, on whom he depended, wrote, 'The torture he was in is not to be described. Five persons could scare hold him for a week from tearing out his own eyes' (v, 207). He survived another three years walking up to ten hours a day round the great deanery, his mind gone. For a century or more it was thought that Swift was mad until the true nature of his lifelong suffering was discovered and Sir William Wilde (father of Oscar), after three years of research, wrote: 'Swift was not, at any period of his life, not even in his last illness, what is understood as mad' (*38*, 213).

Almost his last recorded words are to be found in a letter by his cousin Deane Swift of 4 April 1744: 'This puts me in mind of what he said about five days ago. He endeavoured several times to speak to his servant (now and then he calls him by his name). At last, not finding words to express what he would be at, after some uneasiness, he said "I am a fool"' (v. 215).

Swift eventually died on 19 October 1745 at the age of 78. He was buried three days later in St Patrick's Cathedral. The Latin epitaph he composed for himself was placed over his grave. It speaks of his heart 'lacerated by savage indignation' and exhorts the onlooker to go away and to imitate this strenuous vindicator of liberty. Yeats translated it freely as:

> Swift has sailed into his rest;
> Savage indignation there
> Cannot lacerate his breast.
> Imitate him, if you dare,
> World-besotted traveller; he
> Served human liberty.[4]

Two plaques on the floor of the Cathedral commemorate Swift and Stella. However, over the years these have been frequently moved (as have the coffins and their contents) depending on the different views of successive deans about the relationship between Swift and Stella. So mystery followed Swift even to the grave.

Postscript

Dr Johnson, in his *Lives of the English Poets*, wrote in praise of Swift soon after his death, but it was not long before he was attacked by Macaulay as 'the apostate politician, the ribald priest, the perjured lover, a heart burning with hatred against the whole human race.'[1] In our century Swift has been restored to his rightful place, particularly by the enthusiasm of W.B. Yeats: '... passion enobled by intensity, by endurance, by wisdom. We had it in one man once. He lies in St Patrick's now under the greatest epitaph in history.'[2] Other Irish writers have also shown the influence of Swift, particularly Joyce in 'Gas from a Burner' and 'The Holy Office'.

It is hard to sum him up. We can see that he was not an 'original' writer. Indeed, he would not have wanted to claim such an assessment since with his fellow Augustans he assumed that the things man has received are better than those he has invented. But he was a supreme artist in his ability to 'conjure known things into unexpected things'.[3] His life's work involved much repetition of ideas. His work was all of a piece; whether it was the later Irish polemical writing echoing what he had written thirty years earlier, or his rhetorical trickery in *A Modest Proposal* that he had first employed in *A Tale of a Tub* at the beginning of the century.

However, despite the often apparent arrogance of a man who was convinced he was right and who was always bullying his friends and readers, he did not claim much for his work: 'I write pamphlets and [142] follies merely for amusement, and when they are finished, or I grow weary in the middle, I cast them into the fire, and partly out of dislike and chiefly because I know they will signify nothing' (iv, 434). There is here a genuine and not a feigned modesty, a diffidence. Yet Swift was privately delighted by the success of so much of his work as we see from comments in his letters.

He was a disturber. His fundamental scepticism simply would not allow him to take things for granted and he wanted to make the world do the same. He was not, I think, a misanthrope, nor was he a cynic, nor was he really a pessimist. But he was extremely honest. He was so honest that he had to tell the truth even when polite society or current fashionable philosophies decreed otherwise. On Ireland, for example, he could not dissemble: 'Swift's anger was always divided between the stupidity of the Irish and the rapacity of the English.'[4] He called himself 'an examiner only and not a reformer', (III, 82) but this was too modest a claim. He was also very impassioned and Yeats rightly wrote in 'Blood and the Moon' of

Swift beating on his breast in sibylline frenzy blind
Because the heart in his blood-sodden breast had
    dragged him down into mankind.[5]

T.S. Eliot described this in calmer terms:

. . . the conscious impotence of rage
At human folly, and the laceration
Of laughter at what ceases to amuse.[6]

Such a man could never, any more than Yeats himself could, 'Cast a cold eye on life, on death'.

Yeats was also surely right in drawing our attention to the solitary quality of Swift's life and, like Johnson when *he* was alone, Swift, being as profound a Christian and moralist as Johnson, had no need to [143] dissemble. Swift expressed his concerns in prayer: 'You have given me wisdom to know myself a fool, without the humility to suffer foolishness in peace. You have commanded me to love my neighbour as myself, yet self-love is at the centre of my affection . . . You have given me anger and pity, yet I know not how to apply them. O Lord, take not my reason from me . . . Let me not live to be dependent . . . Lord, let me die a whole man.'

Fortunately, today, we can look on Swift with all his failings and yet see so much that is attractive. With Yeats we can also say, 'Swift haunts me; he is always round the next corner.'[7]

References

Chapter 2: The Prince of Journalists (pp. 36—60)
1. *Lives of the English Poets*, volume II, Oxford 1959, 213.
2. *Ibid.*, 208.
3. *Jonathan Swift*, London 1965, 65.

Chapter 3: The Hibernian Patriot (pp. 61—86)
1. *Collected Plays*, London 1953, 613.
2. *Collected Poems*, London 1955, 301.
3. *Lives of the English Poets*, 210.
4. 'Introduction to *The Words Upon the Window-Pane*' (1934) in *Explorations*, London 1962, 348.
5. Letter to Sir Hercules Langrishe (3 January 1792) in *The Writings and Speeches of Edmund Burke*, London n.d., volume 4, 305.

Chapter 4: The World-Besotted Traveller (pp. 87—111)
1. *Fact and Fiction*, London 1961, 32.
2. 'The political significance of *Gulliver's Travels*', *Proceedings of the British Academy*, IX (1919—20), 237—59.
3. Quoted in Matthew Hodgart, *'Gulliver's Travels'* in Denis Donoghue, ed., *Swift Remembered*, Cork 1968, 35—6.
4. See Jeremiah Hogan, *The English Language in Ireland*, Dublin 1927.
5. Hodgart, 39.
6. *Gulliver's Travels* (Studies in English Literature), London 1968, 52.

Chapter 5: A Poisoned Rat in a Hole (pp. 112—140)
1. Quoted in *Lives of the English Poets*, 218.
2. Quoted in *Lives of the English Poets*, 207.
3. Thomas Sheridan, *The Life of the Rev. Dr. Jonathan Swift*, London 1784, 280.
4. *Collected Poems*, 277.

Postscript (pp. 141–143))

1. Macaulay, reviewing Lord Mahon's *History of the War of* [145] *Succession in Spain* in the *Edinburgh Review*, Jan. 1833, vol. LVI, 538.
2. *The Letters of W.B. Yeats*, ed. Allan Wade, London 1954, 776.
3. J.J. Hogan, 'Bicentenary of Jonathan Swift 1667–1745' in A. Norman Jeffares, ed., *Swift* (Modern Judgements), London 1969, 52.
4. *Drapier's Letters*, ed. Herbert Davis, Oxford 1935, intro. xi.
5. *Collected Poems*, 268.
6. 'Little Gidding', *Four Quartets*, London 1959, 54.
7. *Explorations*, 345.

Select Bibliography

Swift's Own Work

Prose Writings of Jonathan Swift, ed. Herbert Davis, Oxford 1939—58. Quotations from these fourteen volumes are indicated by the volume number (I—XIV) followed by page number(s).

The Correspondence of Jonathan Swift, ed. Harold Williams, Oxford 1963—5. Quotations from these five volumes are indicated by the volume number (i—v) followed by page number(s).

The Poetry of Jonathan Swift, ed. Harold Williams, Oxford 1937. Quotations from these three volumes are indicated by the volume number (I—III) followed by the page number(s).

Journal to Stella, ed. Harold Williams, Oxford 1948. Quotations from these two volumes are indicated by 'JS' followed by volume and page number(s).

Books about Swift

I have deliberately chosen a selected list since the reader who wants to read further will have no difficulty finding other titles. I have divided the titles into sections covering various aspects of Swift's life and work for ease of reference. The books are numbered and references in the text are to these numbers followed by page references.

Swift's Life

1. Ehrenpreis, Irvin, *Swift: The Man, His Works and the Age, I: Mr Swift and His Contemporaries*, London 1962.
2. Ehrenpreis, Irvin, *Swift, The Man His Works and the Age, II: Dr Swift*, London 1967.
3. Johnston, Denis, *In Search of Swift*, Dublin 1959. A rather quirky investigation of aspects of Swift's life and particularly the much argued questions of his 'marriage' to Stella and his relationship with Vanessa. But fascinating reading.

Swift and Ireland

4. Beckett, J.C., 'Swift and the Anglo-Irish tradition' in C.J. [147]
   Rawson, ed., *Focus: Swift*, London 1971, 155–70.

5. Ferguson, Oliver W., *Jonathan Swift and Ireland*, Urbana,
   Illinois 1962. A full account of all Swift's Irish writings
   set against the background.

6. Jarrell, Mackie L., '"Jack and the Dane": Swift traditions
   in Ireland', in A.N. Jeffares, ed., *Fair Liberty Was All His
   Cry: A Tercentenary Tribute to Jonathan Swift,
   1667–1745*, London and New York 1967. A fascinating
   account of the numerous folk tales concerning Swift cir-
   culating in Ireland for many years after his death.

7. Johnston, Edith Mary, *Ireland in the Eighteenth Century*,
   Dublin 1974. A handy paperback volume in the Gill
   History of Ireland series which gives an excellent account
   of the background to Swift.

8. Landa, Louis A., *Swift and the Church of Ireland*, Oxford
   1954. A full account of Swift's lifelong involvement with
   the Church.

9. Mercier, Vivian, *The Irish Comic Tradition*, Oxford 1962.
   Chapter 7 discusses Swift and the Anglo-Irish tradition.

10. Mercier, Vivian, 'Swift and the Gaelic Tradition' in Jeffares
    (see 6 above), 279–89.

11. Ross, Angus, 'The Hibernian Patriot's apprenticeship', in
    Clive T. Probyn, ed., *The Art of Jonathan Swift*, London
    1978, 83–107.

Swift and Women

12. Davis, Herbert, *Stella: A Gentlewoman of the Eighteenth
    Century*, New York 1942. A sympathetic discussion of
    the relationship between Swift and Stella.

13. Paulson, Ronald, 'Swift, Stella and permanence', *Journal
    of English Literary History* XXVII (1960), 298–314.

14. Woolf, Virginia, 'Swift's *Journal to Stella*' in her *Second
    Common Reader*, London 1935. An early and sympathetic
    analysis of Stella.

Aspects of Swift

15. Brown, Norman O., 'The excremental vision' in Ernest
    Tuveson ed., *Swift*, Englewood Cliffs, New Jersey 1964,
    31–54. A highly controversial but fascinating discussion
    of Swift and scatology.

16. Foot, Michael, *The Pen and the Sword*, London 1957. A
    very readable account of Swift's campaign against the
    Duke of Marlborough.

17. Orwell, George, 'Politics versus literature' in Sonia Orwell and Ian Angus, ed., *The Collected Essays, Journalism and Letters of George Orwell*, London 1968.

[148]

Swift's Poetry
There have been a number of books recently written about Swift's poetry, but they are largely unsatisfactory. Two recent books are listed below as well as a controversial essay about the apparent 'anti-poetry' of Swift.

18. Fischer, I., *On Swift's Poetry*, Florida 1978.
19. Jaffe, N.C., *The Poet Swift*, Hanover, New Hampshire 1977.
20. San Juan, E., 'The anti-poetry of Jonathan Swift', *Philological Quarterly* XLIV (1965), 387—96.

'Gulliver's Travels'
21. Brady, Frank, ed., *Twentieth Century Interpretations of 'Gulliver's Travels'*, Englewood Cliffs, New Jersey 1968.
22. Case, A.E., *Four Essays on 'Gulliver's Travels'*, Princeton 1945.
23. Donoghue, Denis, 'The brainwashing of Gulliver', *The Listener*, 96, 4 November 1976, 578—9.
24. Gravil, R., ed., *'Gulliver's Travels'* (Casebook series), London 1974.
25. Lock, F.P., *The Politics of 'Gulliver's Travels'*, Oxford 1980.
26. Peake, Charles, 'The coherence of *Gulliver's Travels*', in C.J. Rawson, ed., *Focus: Swift*, London 1971, 171—96. A succinct summary of the various arguments and about Book Four in particular.

Other Works
27. Cook, Richard I., *Jonathan Swift as a Tory Pamphleteer*, Seattle and London 1967.
28. Hall, Basil, '"An inverted hypocrite": Swift the churchman', in Brian Vickers, ed., *The World of Jonathan Swift*, Oxford 1968, 38—68.
29. Harth, Philip, *Swift and Anglican Rationalism: The Religious Background of 'A Tale of a Tub'*, Chicago 1961.
30. Johnson, J.W., 'Swift's historical outlook', in A.N. Jeffares, ed., *Swift: Modern Judgements*, London 1968, 96—120.
31. Speck, W.A., '*The Examiner* examined: Swift's Tory pamphleteering', in C.J. Rawson, ed., *Focus: Swift*, London 1971, 138—54.

32. Traugott, John, *'A Tale of a Tub'*, in C.J. Rawson (see 31 above), 76—120. [149]

General Works

33. Bullitt, John M., *Jonathan Swift and the Anatomy of Satire: A Study of Satiric Technique*, Cambridge, Mass. 1953.
34. Davis, Herbert, *The Satire of Jonathan Swift*, New York 1947.
35. Donoghue, Denis, *Jonathan Swift: A Critical Introduction*, Cambridge 1969.
36. Ehrenpreis, Irvin, *The Personality of Jonathan Swift*, London 1958. A pioneering study of important questions about Swift: madness, obscenity, women, old age.
37. Ewald, W.B., *The Masks of Jonathan Swift*, Oxford 1954.
38. Foot, Michael, 'Round the next corner: the pursuit of Jonathan Swift', in his *Debts of Honour*, London 1980, 198—233. A spirited discussion.
39. Price, Martin, *Swift's Rhetorical Art*, London 1963.
40. Quintana, Ricardo, *The Mind and Art of Jonathan Swift*, London 1936.
41. Rawson, C.J., *Gulliver and The Gentle Reader: Studies in Swift and Our Time*, London 1973. A rewarding discussion of Swift and others.
42. Reilly, Patrick, *Jonathan Swift: The Brave Desponder*, Manchester 1982. Likely to become a major discussion of Swift's work; particularly good on relations with other writers.
43. Rosenheim, Edward, Jr., *Swift and The Satirist's Art*, Chicago 1963.
44. Speck, W.A., *Swift* (Literature in Perspective), London 1969.
45. Ward, David, *Jonathan Swift, An Introductory Essay*, London 1973. Perhaps the best short (paperback) introduction to Swift.
46. Williams, Kathleen, *Jonathan Swift and the Age of Compromise*, Lawrence, Kansas 1958. A long established major discussion of Swift.

Index

Addison, Joseph, 20, 36, 41, 47

Anne, Queen, 32, 41, 42, 44, 48, 49, 51, 52, 59, 60

Arbuthnot, Dr John, 52, 59, 67, 116, 130, 138

Argument against abolishing Christianity, 38-9

Ashe, St George, 6, 63

'Ballad on the Game of Traffick', 28-9

'Bank thrown down, The', 76

Battle of the Books, 13, 14

'Baucis and Philemon', 36

Beckett, Samuel, 33

Bentley, Richard, 13, 14

'Beautiful Young Nymph going to Bed, A', 131, 132

Berkeley, George, Bishop, 114

Berkeley, Charles, Earl of, 21, 23, 25, 28

Bettesworth, Richard, 126-7

Bickerstaff Papers, 37

birthday poems to Stella, 66-8, 112-3

Boulter, Archbishop Hugh, 76, 85

Brecht, Bertolt, *The Life of Galilei*, 103

Burke, Edmund, 70

'Cadenus and Vanessa', 56-8

Carolan (Turlough O Carolan), 129

Carteret, John Baron, 81, 82, 83, 100

'Cassinus and Peter', 132-4

Causes of the Wretched Conditions of Ireland, 123-5

Chetwode, Knightley, 63, 138

Conduct of the Allies, The, 48-9, 55

Cosgreve, William, 20

Cobbett, William, 45

Contests and Dissensions between the Nobles and the Commons, 25-6, 28

Cutts, John, Baron, 33

Dampier, William, *Voyage round the World*, 89

Davitt, Michael, 70

Defoe, Daniel, *Robinson Crusoe*, 89-90

Delany, Dr Patrick, 65, 114, 125, 129

'Description of a City Shower, A', 41-2

'Description of an Irish Feast, The', 129

'Description of the Morning, A', 36-7, 41

'Description of a Salamander, The', 33, 34

Dingley, Rebecca, 12, 27, 61, 64, 89, 139

Directions to Servants, 130-1

Donoghue, Denis, 96, 134

Dr Steevens's Hospital, 114

Drapier's Letters, The, 30, 46, 69, 73, *76-85*

Dryden, John, 3, 4, 13, 14

Ehrenpreis, Irvin, 10, 58

'Elegy on Mr Patrige, An', 75

Eliot, T. S., 142

England, Church of, 15, 16, 26-7, 30-1, 32, 39
Examiner Papers, 44-6, 48, 49, 59, 104
'Excellent New Song, An', 75

'Fable of Midas, The', 49-50
First Fruits, 32, 34, 35, 36, 40, 41, 43, 44
Firth, Sir Charles, 100
Foot, Michael, 45, 70, 91
Ford, Charles, 41, 61, 72, 90, 116

Gay, John, 59, 91, 116, 130, 138; *The Beggar's Opera*, 117
George I, King, 44, 61, 76, 111
Germain, Lady Betty (*née* Berkeley), 22, 28, 116
Godolphin, Sidney, Earl of, 42-3
Golding, William, *The Lord of the Flies*, 98
Grattan family, 63, 114
Grattan, Henry, 63, 70
Gulliver's Travels, 2, 6, 19, 33, 36, 38, *68-73, 87-110*, 120, 131-2

Harding, John, 80, 82, 83, 84
Harley, Robert (Earl of Oxford), 30, 41, 43, 44, 47, 48, 51, 52, 54, 59, 60, 63, 95, 100
History of the Four Last Years of the Queen, 54-5
Hobbes, Thomas, 32, 106
Hodgart, Matthew, 110
Hogarth, William, 129
'Holyhead, September 25th 1727', 111
'Humble Petition of Mrs Frances Harris, The', 22

'In Sickness', 62
Intelligencer, The, 117-18
'Ireland', 111
Ireland, Church of, 9-11, 22-4, 32, 34, 41, 43-4, 55, 126
Ireland, state of, 119-20
'Irish Bishops, On the', 126

James II, King, 22, 26, 30
Johnson, Esther ('Stella'), 8, 12-13, 27, 40, 41, 49, 56, 58, 61, 63-4, 65, 66-8, 88-9, 111, 112-14, 116, 131, 136, 140
Johnson, Samuel, 46, 53, 69, 134, 141, 142-3
Journal to Stella, 46-7, 54
Joyce, James, 33, 141

Kendal, Duchess of, 76, 81
Kilkenny School, 5-6
Kilroot, 9, 10, 11
King, William, Archbishop, 22, 29, 35, 48, 56, 61, 63, 66, 73, 75, 77, 82-3

'Lady's Dressing Room, The', 132, 135
Laracor, 23, 27, 29, 39, 41
La Rochefoucault, Duc de, 136
'Legion Club, The', 100, 127-9, 135
Letter concerning the Sacramental Test, A, 29-30
Letter to a Young Gentleman, A, 53-4
Locke, John, 106, 135; *The Reasonableness of Christianity*, 16
Lyon, Dr John, 64, 139

Macaulay, Lord, 141
Marlborough, John, Duke of, 28, 45, 46, 48, 49-51, 55
Marlborough, Sarah, Duchess of, 28, 48, 49
Marsh, Narcissus, 6, 22
Masham, Lady (Abigail Hill), 48, 51, 52, 54
masks, 1, 12, 17, 27, 78, 85
Mechanical Operation of the Spirit, The, 13
Ménières disease, 8, 39, 65-6, 138
Molyneux, William, 70, 74, 81; *The Case of Ireland's being bound*, 71-2
Modest Proposal, A, 38, 46, 119, *120-3*, 141

Moor Park, 7, 8, 9, 11, 12, 13, 27, 28, 34-5
Motte, Benjamin, 90
Murry, J. M., 131

Newton, Sir Isaac, 79

O'Brien, Flann, 33
On the Death of Mrs Johnson, 12, 113-14
'On the Trinity', 106
'On the Words — Brother Protestants, and Fellow Christians', 126
Ormonde, James, Duke of, 54, 63
Ormonde family, 3, 5, 6
Orwell, George, 45; *1984*, 98

'Panegyrick on the Dean, A', 115-16
Parnell, Thomas, 59
Partridge, John, 37
Patrick, 47, 54
peace, 103-4
Phillips, Ambrose, 36
'Phillis, Or, the Progress of Love', 132
Polite Conversation, 130
politics, English, 26-7, 30-2, 34, 36, 39, 40, 41, 42-50, 55, 59-60, 63, 91, 99-103, 111
politics, Irish, 29-30, 61-86, 127-9
Pope, Alexander, 2, 17, 59, 62, 67, 69, 74, 86, 87, 88, 106, 111, 113, 116, 118, 135, 138
Prior, Matthew, 20, 36
'Progress of Beauty, The', 132
'Progress of Marriage, The', 132
Proposal for Correcting the English Tongue, 52-3
Proposal for giving Badges to the Beggars, 125
Proposal for the Universal Use of Irish Manufacture, 72-5, 77, 124

Redmond, John, 70
Reilly, Patrick, 94, 98
religion, 15-17, 29-32, 38-9, 125

Rogers, Woodes, *A Cruising Voyage round the World*, 89
Ross, Angus, 110
Royal Society, 14, 105, 120
Russell, Bertrand, 94
St John, Henry (Viscount Bolingbroke), 30, 43, 44, 47, 48, 51, 52, 54, 59, 60, 63, 95, 100, 111, 116, 138
St Patrick's Cathedral, 23, 55, 56, 72, 73, 113, 125, 130, 139-40
St Patrick's Hospital, 114, 138
satire, 117
'Satirical Elegy on the Death of a Late Famous General, A', 50-1
scatological poems, 131-5
Sentiments of a Church-of-England Man, The, 30-2
'Serious Poem upon William Wood, A', 84
Shaw, Bernard, 56
Sheridan, Dr Thomas, 65, 111, 114, 116, 117, 118
Short Character of the Earl of Wharton, 45-6
Short View of the State of Ireland, 86, 119-20
Smedley, Dean Jonathan, 126
Snow, C. P., *The New Men*, 104
Somerset, Elizabeth, Duchess of, 51-2, 60, 106
South Sea Bubble, 75
Spenser, Edmund, *A View of the Present State of Ireland*, 119
Steele, Sir Richard, 20, 36, 47
'Stella' *see* Esther Johnson
Story of the Imjured Lady, The, 34
'Strephon and Chloe', 132-3
Sunderland, Charles, Earl of, 21, 55, 62
Swift, Abigail (mother), 3, 4-5, 11, 25, 40, 41
Swift, Deane (cousin), 139
Swift, Godwin (uncle), 134
Swift, Jane (sister), 5
Swift, Jonathan (father), 3, 4
Swift, Jonathan
    childhood and education, 3-7

at Moor Park, 7-9
first parish, 9-10
meets 'Varina', 11
returns to Moor Park, 11-12
death of Sir William Temple, 21
chaplain to the Earl of Berkeley, 21-2
receives Laracor, 23
ends relationship with 'Varina', 24
visits England, 25
Stella and Mrs Dingley move to Ireland, 27
accession of Queen Anne, 28
in Ireland for three and a half years, 33
to England over the First Fruits, 35
begins relationship with Vanessa, 39
last visit to his mother, 40
in Ireland, 40
returns to England for the First Fruits, 41
edits the *Examiner*, 44
Tory election landslide, 47
writing the *History of the Four Last Years*, 54-5
obtains Deanery of St Patrick's, 55-56
relationship with Vanessa, 56-8
in England for the last days of Queen Anne, 59-60
in Ireland, 61
supposed marriage, 63
relations with Vanessa, 64-5
Wood's Halfpence, 76-86
travels to England, 88
last visit to England, 110-11
Stella's dying days, 112-14
among his friends in Ireland, 114-16
involvement in Irish church politics, 126-9
last days, 138-40
attitude to Ireland and the Irish, 69-70, 73, 107-8, 116
desire for preferment, 9, 22-4
knowledge of Irish, 129-30
letter writing, 116
poetry, 8-9, 13, 22 28-9
'misogyny', 132
scorn for logic and metaphysics, 6
wordplay, 33
Swift, Rev. Thomas (grandfather), 4, 110
Swift, Thomas (cousin), 8, 11, 27
Swift, Thomas (uncle), 3
Swift, William (uncle), 9

Tale of a Tub, A, 13, *14-20*, 34, 51, 141
Temple, Sir William, 3, 7-8, 9, 12, 13, 21, 34, 48, 56
Test Act, 26, 29-30, 31, 39, 126
Thoughts on Religion, 102
Tighe, Richard, 117, 126
Trinity College Dublin, 6, 7, 28, 61, 130

'Vanessa' (see Esther Vanhomrigh)
Vanhomrigh, Esther ('Vanessa'), 39-40, 56-8, 59, 61-2, 64-5, 116, 131
Vanhomrigh, Mrs Hester, 39, 56
'Verses on the Death of Dr Swift', 134-5, 135-7
'Verses on the Upright Judge', 84

Walpole, Horace, 116
Walpole, Sir Robert, 73, 77, 81, 82, 85, 88, 93, 100, 111
Waring, Jane ('Varina'), 11, 13, 24, 40
Wellington, Duke of, 108
Wharton, Thomas, Marquis of, 41, 45-6
When I come to be old 1699, 21
Whitshed, William, 62, 83
'Whitshed's Motto on his Coach', 83
Wilde, Sir William, 139
William III, King, 7, 9, 21, 26, 28, 32
'Windsor Prophecy, The', 51-2
Wood, William, 76-85

[154]

Wood's Halfpence, 29, *76-85*, 94
Wotton, William, 13, 14

'Yahoo's Overthrow, The', 127
Yeats, W.B., 4, 70, 110, 134, 140,
141, 143; 'After Long Silence',
68; 'Blood and the Moon',
142; 'In Memory of Major
Robert Gregory', 136; *Words
Upon the Window Sill*, 66-7